W9-BJT-984

Praise for *Old World Witchcraft*

"Grimassi's approach to witchcraft brings a vitality and vibrancy to this book. He writes with knowledge, the voice of experience, and the exuberance of a passionate belief. Historical beliefs and practices are seamlessly woven into the fabric of contemporary potential. This is a wonderful book, and I have enjoyed it."

—Rev. Paul Beyerl, author of *The Master Book of Herbalism*

"*Old World Witchcraft* opens an exciting new window on the whole subject of witchcraft, revealing such concepts as the organic memory of the earth and veneration of the plant kingdom. This is a refreshing book of new yet ancient wisdom that should not be missed. A true delight."

—Raymond Buckland, author of *The Witch Book*

"Raven Grimassi has single-handedly put the witch back into the Craft with this book. *Old World Witchcraft* is real magic for real witches— and a must have for every serious practitioner!"

—Dorothy Morrison, author of *Utterly Wicked*

"Exposing the Old World witch is no easy task, but after meticulousness research, Grimassi uncovers the real historical witch behind the modern day image. Misconceptions are washed away as the witch of the past is unveiled—a common member of society with uncommon skills and an exceptional understanding of the world about. The inclusion of a modern grimoire embellishes this work and brings to the forefront modern practices of significantly older beliefs. *Old World Witchcraft* is a generous introduction to a modern practice and its ancient origins."

—Andrew Theitic, editor of *The Witches' Almanac*

"*Old World Witchcraft* is destined to be a classic and an agent of change that helps witchcraft regain its position of respect and honor in Paganism and the general community. It is intellectual and spiritual water extinguishing the burning-time flames of hypocrisy. In this amazing book, Raven introduces the reader to the original image of the powerful, respected, and feared witch while detangling the centuries of false illusions, hysteria, and 'spiritual ethnocide.' Read and take a trip into the true soul of the witch."

—Orion Foxwood, co-founder of the House of Brigh Faery
Seership Institute and author of *The Tree of Enchantment*

"Any worker of magic/k will find much inspiration in Raven Grimassi's *Old World Witchcraft*. The chapter 'Witches: The Plant People' is especially intriguing. If the aspiring Green Witch only adopts using 'charged water' for her plants, or establishes a 'Shadow Garden'—a kind of magical compost heap of non-toxic organic materials left over from rituals—or meditates on Grimassi's reflections on mortar and pestle magic/k, she will have more than recouped the price of the book."

—Judith Hawkins-Tillirson, author of
The Weiser Concise Guide to Herbal Magick

"In *Old World Witchcraft*, Raven Grimassi effectively strips away the thin veneer of the Wiccan revival to give us credible insight into the truth about the practice of real witches. From a deep understanding of the secret powers of nature, to the ancient magical powers of the moon, to communion with otherworldly beings and the spirits of the dead, the witch is a timeless and mysterious creature. Within these pages, Grimassi opens the doorway to the witch's cottage, hidden deep within the forest of our consciousness, that we may be blessed by the witch's wisdom once more."

—Christian Day, Salem warlock and author of
The Witches' Book of the Dead

"It is important for witches to understand our origins, especially as we facilitate the dawning of a new age. This wise book can help us appreciate who we are. Exquisitely researched, it also thoroughly refutes the ridiculous charges that have historically been made against us."

—Eileen Holland, author of *The Wicca Handbook*
and *The Spellcaster's Reference*

"I admire bravery and creativity, and Raven Grimassi's *Old World Witchcraft* has both in abundance. In a time when many practitioners fawn over the so-called fickle truth of academic perspectives on witchcraft, Raven brings forth mythic truth on what it is to be a witch. This book was written for those who have a vocation to be witches and wish for a path that is modern but whose roots are watered with the essence of the old lore. *Old World Witchcraft* is a perfect remedy for the disenchanted seeker who is lost in the world of the literalists and looking for the path home to mystery."

—Ivo Dominguez, author of *Spirit Speak*
and *Casting Sacred Space*

"Grimassi brings together an impressive array of threads from folklore, scholarly literature, history, and experience, gifting us with a tapestry—a vibrant picture of the Old Craft of the Wise."

—T. Thorn Coyle, teacher and author of *Kissing the Limitless*

"On a journey to our magickal past in the Old World to create our future, I can think of no better guide than Raven Grimassi. His experience, scholarship, and, most importantly, wisdom shines through these pages, illuminating anyone's serious practice of witchcraft."

—Christopher Penczak, author of the
Temple of Witchcraft series and *The Plant Spirit Familiar*

OLD WORLD
WITCHCRAFT

ANCIENT WAYS FOR MODERN DAYS

RAVEN GRIMASSI

WEISERBOOKS
San Francisco, CA / Newburyport, MA

First published in 2011 by Weiser Books, an imprint of
Red Wheel/Weiser, LLC
665 Third Street, Suite 400
San Francisco, CA 94107
www.redwheelweiser.com

Copyright © 2011 by Raven Grimassi
All rights reserved. No part of this publication may be reproduced or transmitted in any form or by any means, electronic or mechanical, including
photocopying, recording, or by any information storage and retrieval system,
without permission in writing from Red Wheel/Weiser, LLC. Reviewers may
quote brief passages.

ISBN: 978-1-57863-505-4
Library of Congress Cataloging-in-Publication Data is available upon request.

Cover design: Jim Warner
Cover photograph: *Mandragora officinarum* by Benjamin A. Vierling /
    www.bvierling.com
Interior: Jane Hagaman

Illustrations on pp. 81, 97, 127, 133, 213–216, 229, and 231
    by Diane Haynes.
Plant illustrations on pp. 113–120, 143, and 217 © Dover.
Witch's Mark illustration on p. 155 and plant spirit symbols on p. 209
    by Raven Grimassi.
Altar photo on p. 163 and apple talisman photo on p. 221
    by Stephanie Taylor-Grimassi.

Typeset in Goudy Oldstyle, Trajan, and Chantilly
Printed in Canada
TCP
10 9 8 7 6 5 4 3 2 1
The paper used in this publication meets the minimum requirements of the
American National Standard for Information Sciences—Permanence of
Paper for Printed Library Materials Z39.48-1992 (R1997).

Dedicated to all who suffered
torment, pain, or death for what they believed,
or for what others believed about them.

Contents

Preface

This book is a departure from the familiar theme of arguing for witchcraft as the survival of an ancient tradition. The system presented in the following chapters is not that of the pacifist adhering to the Wiccan guidelines of the "harm none" Rede. Then what is this book about? Simply stated, it is about old forms of witchcraft traceable through aged European roots. But it is also about the mystical *Old World* and the witches who lived it and live it still.

I will touch on themes that appear in modern witchcraft and Wicca such as a goddess and god figure. In doing so I am only examining references past and present in a search for equilibrium. I am not trying to make a case for witchcraft as a pre-Gardnerian religion that survived into modern times. If you simply follow along to discover where I take things (without assuming anything in advance), then pleasant surprises await. I will not lure you into becoming entangled in the brambles; instead we will walk the path together for a midnight visit in the old witches' garden.

This book is written in the belief that witches have existed as real people for countless centuries. But these are not the witches of Neo-Pagan romantic ideas, and they are not the stereotypes of the diabolical witch in league with the Devil of Judeo-Christian theology. In many ways the witch appearing in this book is one about whom very little has been written at all.

It is my view that no official history of witchcraft truly exists. This is because the "history" presented by the academic community is not the depiction of any real society of people known as witches. Instead it is the study of non-witches and their views about what they referred to as witchcraft and witches. Academic history in this field is the story of how superstition influenced popular beliefs about imaginary witches and witchcraft, and how theologians further invented ideas about the subject. This is a make-believe witchcraft of fantasy themes, and not an ethnographical study of a real culture of people who were witches. If we are to call this history, then I feel we need to note that it is a mythical history at best.

It is possible, of course, that some people were involved in diabolical practices involving satanic worship, but could they have numbered in the tens of thousands across all of Europe? This seems unlikely. If we are to regard the number of people charged with witchcraft over the centuries as an accurate reflection of the sect's numbers, however, then we must say yes. But what we are saying "yes" to is the portrayal of witches by people who believed witches could fly, change into animal form, and frolic in person with demons. How credible can these "authorities" be in such a light? Personally, I have to question their ability to reason and therefore their aptitude for understanding the facts and fantasies regarding the matter before them.

In contrast to the "learned view" of the authorities, I believe that looking at the folkloric witch of the "uneducated people" brings us one step closer to uncovering the witch (free of themes that support an agenda). The problem here is that what we are looking at is superstition and how fear instead of reality shapes the belief of a people. The academic presentation is the view of witches by people who feared and hated them. It is not the account of people who actually knew authentic witches in their community and conversed with them about their beliefs and practices. Oddly, it is the beliefs of outsiders that scholars draw upon to present the history of witches and witchcraft.

Anything compared against the academic picture of witchcraft that does not comply is called pseudo-history, but how can we have a fake history of witchcraft when we do not possess a factual one? Many Neo-Pagan writers, myself included, have been charged with creating pseudo-history when writing about views related to the roots of modern witchcraft and Wicca. Some writers believe in the existence of a pre-Christian religion of witches who venerated a goddess such as Diana, and one that survived in some fashion well into the Christian era. Critics respond that if such a thing existed there would be evidence in the witch trials.

References to venerating Diana and other goddesses do show up in trial records and those of the Inquisition.[1] Therefore we have no absence of the concept (not to mention the existence of an ancient literary tradition associating goddesses with witchcraft). This, by itself, is not proof of goddess worship among the accused, but neither is it something to completely dismiss if we are to be fair and balanced. The figure of a goddess does appear in witch trials throughout Europe. Why is that?

My purpose in this book is not to argue for the survival of a witches' religion from pre-Christian times. Instead the goal of this book is to allow what I call the "Old Ways" witch figure to emerge by clearing away the large mounds of debris that surround it. There is difficulty in offering a finite definition of what I believe constitutes such a witch. A witch uses magic, but so too does a sorceress or ceremonial magician. Divination is one of the arts of witchcraft, but there are people who use divination and are not witches. A witch can believe in many deities and spirits, but this is also common among pagans. Pagans are not witches. Witches use herbs for magical purposes but so too do non-witches.

My personal belief is that what separates the witch from non-witches is the mystical alignment of the witch. It is in the "enchanted worldview" of the witch that we can find a definition for her or him. Here we see that the witch believes in a consciousness that inhabits all things. Rocks, plants, and trees have consciousness, or they are shelters for a variety of sentient spirit beings. This is evidenced in the belief that objects possess specific power that can be used in a spell or ritual. From this perspective the witch works with an occult set of correspondences. If objects possessed only raw power, then any single one would serve any spell. The fact that a particular object delivers a specialized effect indicates that the object possesses a consciousness of its nature that allows it to do so (or such is the occult tenet).

Continuing with the definition of the witch, she or he has a rapport with spirits or other nonmaterial beings. The witch works intimately with the "Otherworld" and can communicate with souls of the dead. One specific group of beings that witches work with is the Faery race. These are not cute little fairies of popular children's tales; they are ancient and powerful beings who reportedly existed long before humankind.

Perhaps more so than any other single marker, the art of magic denotes the witch. This magic is lunar in nature and is associated with the night. Naturally the magic of the witch is not limited to the nighttime; it can be performed under a sunny sky as well. However, the moon is essential to the witch, and without this primary component, a person is not a witch in the traditional sense or in the Old Ways understanding.

The last part of my definition of the witch points to the forest or woodlands. This is the primal home of the witch. From the deep dark places of the forest arose the spiritual-mindedness of the witch. If we can say that the witch possesses a theology, then it lies in the experience of the forest. Here not only grow the traditional plants of witchcraft, but it is from the forest that primitive ideas about the witches' *deities* first formed. This is covered in full detail later in the book.

In the following pages we will uncover what I call the "Old Ways Witch." I am not claiming that he or she is the survivor of an unbroken tradition passed down intact from ancient times. What I intend to demonstrate is that the ways of witchcraft described in this book are very old. Their age is not important, but what they represent is of value because they are part of the spiritual lineage of those witches who today practice a rooted form of witchcraft.

I think of the *Craft* as a great old tree. The roots nourish a tree, and they hold the tree in place to secure it against forces that would otherwise topple it. The new growth on the tree and its buds, flowers, and seeds come forth to allow for a new generation of trees. The DNA is the soul of the tree, and the Old Ways witch is the bearer of this vital strand.

What follows in this book is what I believe about witches and witchcraft and the reasons why I believe what I do. It is not my story alone, for I impart what many Old Ways witches have shared with me over the years. For me these ways are the things worthy of preserving and passing on.

Introduction

The topic of witchcraft is quite a tangled ball of string. This applies to the views of scholars as well as those of Neo-Pagans. Much "undoing" and "unlearning" is required in order to remove obstacles that stand in the way of a balanced perspective. I do not personally believe that the truth about witchcraft and witches can be sorted out to everyone's satisfaction. But I do feel that we can and should move now to higher ground for a clearer perspective.

My own views about the subject of witchcraft have changed somewhat over time, and I am not embarrassed to admit it. Some people seem to keep an author frozen in time and do not allow for growth and maturity of vision over the years. That is an unfortunate fact, but I am optimistic that the majority of people welcome new insights from those of us who have been around longer than we care to think about.

My own study of published materials about witchcraft began in the late 1960s. I have devoted the last four decades of my life to in-depth study and research in this field. My approach has been to read academic works, folkloric studies, ancient literature, occult writings, and a wide variety of books by practitioners of witchcraft and Wiccan systems. My efforts have not involved working on my research and study now and then as one might do in taking time for a favorite hobby. My work in the field of witchcraft always remained a priority. I can honestly say that no week ever passed over all these years without countless hours of focused attention to my studies of witchcraft material.

My devotion to witchcraft themes brought me into contact with many interesting people over the years. Most of them are witches, but some are mystics, magicians, shamans, and Faery workers. Among the witches I have met, some of my most cherished times were spent with what I call "Old World" or "Old Ways" witches. They are difficult to describe in a way that distinguishes them from other witches. It is more how their presence *feels* than it is specifically any one thing in particular. In the following chapters I will refer to the system as Old World witchcraft and to its practitioners as Old Ways witches.

The primary goal of this book is to share the beliefs and practices of Old World witchcraft. I intentionally avoid calling this form "traditional witchcraft," even though much may be shared in common. Many people view traditional witchcraft as something pertaining to the British Isles, or so it seems from viewing Internet websites and forums. Others define it as having roots in the lore of Lilith, Cain, and Lucifer. With the exception of Lucifer (as a Roman god) these roots are not native to Europe. The Lucifer who appears in traditional witchcraft systems is a very different entity from the one originating in Southern Europe. Later we will look at the blending of witchcraft with Lucifer as viewed in certain systems.

The Old World witchcraft that I present here embraces pre-Christian European themes and does not knowingly incorporate imported beliefs from the general Middle East region. I am not, however, claiming that the system in this book is a surviving tradition from ancient times. I am also not stating that in the past this system was whole and complete in the manner depicted in this book. I simply wish to share a system I know to exist today whose practitioners believe is rooted in very old forms of European witchcraft practices and beliefs.

In the forthcoming chapters I explore the depiction of the witch figure as presented in academic books with such titles as the "history of witchcraft" (in one region or another). In works like these we find the stereotypical witch as an evil person practicing harmful magic. She or he is also engaged in diabolical acts, perverted rituals, and enters into pacts with the Devil. I do not believe that such a sect of witches actually existed in the Middle Ages and Renaissance periods, which is where much of the information about these academic views of witchcraft is based. There may have been individuals involved in some form of practice resembling the diabolical rituals mentioned, but certainly not in the numbers that would merit so many trials throughout all of Europe.

We should note that witchcraft in the Christian era was essentially a crime of heresy, which indicates that the people accused of witchcraft were considered to be Christian. The witches I write about in this book were not Christians and are not today (I refer to the absence of heartfelt Christian beliefs and faith as opposed to putting on a veneer). Although the vast amount of people accused of witchcraft were not even magic-users of any kind, it is likely a small percentage did practice some type of magic. It is also likely that an occasional witch was captured as well, for some of the background lore in trial transcripts appears to reflect elements of Old World witchcraft from previous periods. But of course my definition of a witch is not in keeping with the position of the contemporary academic community. The problem of what properly defines a witch is at the heart of this book.

In chapter one I explore what I call the hushed voices of the past. This is an examination of the roots of the witch figure by focusing on etymology and pre-Christian literary themes. It is the background material that I feel is important here because these are the "building blocks" of period witch lore. The stories themselves I regard as political, but the settings, tools, and other details in these tales can be revealing about authentic practices of the period. Good fiction contains known elements as well as imaginary ones. So in this regard I believe the accounts are useful.

Chapter one also brings to light the process of one culture dominating another. This can and does happen to the degree that one culture displaces another or suppresses another into a seemingly nonexistent status (past or present). Some scholars refer to the latter as submerged or subaltern cultures. Most of the official views of a culture come from an acceptance of the dominating or hegemonic standards, which are regarded as indicative of what identifies or authenticates elements of any given society. The prevailing components of contemporary regional beliefs and practices are often used to dismiss the cultural authenticity of seemingly incongruent beliefs and practices within a given culture. By comparison most scholars reject the views of the submerged cultures because they do not match those of mainstream society. In other words, the subculture is not considered to reflect or preserve surviving elements of the conquered culture in which it once held its place. Scholars typically regard the claims of subaltern societies to be modern inventions, and the substantiating data that support such claims are rejected as being nothing more than anomalies.

In chapter two I explore the stereotype of the evil witch figure, which involves looking at its evolution during the Middle Ages and Renaissance period. I stress the fact that the witch in these periods is a concoction. The examination includes how theologians grafted the Judeo-Christian figure of Satan onto witchcraft. Over the course of many centuries, the Church and its agents constructed a new idea of witchcraft that included diabolical rites performed at the Sabbat. The latter evolves from earlier ideas about witches gathering at the crossroads at night to communicate with the dead.

I also touch upon the views of Neo-Paganism in a section titled "Romancing the Witch." It looks at the popular impressions from the 1800s through to modern times. These views belong to the history of the attitudes about witchcraft and should therefore be considered as part of the complete picture. This section helps to bring the past and present into better focus and allows us an improved understanding about what is inherited versus entirely invented.

In various chapters I explore and reveal elements of what is often regarded as entirely modern ideas related to witchcraft. I refer in particular to the notion of a goddess and god of the witches. My purpose in doing so is twofold. First, I offer old literary and historical references to a goddess of the witches, and I do so simply to demonstrate that the notion itself is ancient. The basic concept is not a Neo-Pagan invention. For the record, my intent is not to argue that ancient witches worshipped a goddess. My presentation of the references is meant to raise the questions that may call for a reexamination of our current views (whether pro or con).

Second, the presentation of themes related to witchcraft deities is meant to show their place and role in modern witchcraft systems. My personal belief is that ancient witches connected more with the idea of "conscious forces" than with that of refined deity concepts. Throughout the book, I present both ideas with the intent of suggesting an evolution as opposed to a complete invention. If there is no historical lineage, we should use caution not to overlook a spiritual one.

One modern model of a witchcraft system described in the book is known as Ash, Birch, and Willow (ABW). I present facets of this system to reveal a view of how balance can be achieved between the allegations of "complete invention" and claims of a surviving tradition of pre-Christian witchcraft. My goal is to demonstrate that something can be ancient and new all at the same time. It must be made clear that ABW is not a surviving tradition from ancient times, but it may be what one could look like in a world where such a thing happened. That being said, this book is not about ABW; it is about persisting themes of Old World witchcraft and how they are practiced today.

Chapter three focuses on removing the negative stereotypes related to witches and witchcraft that arose during the Middle Ages and Renaissance periods (and which persist today in mainstream culture). Attention is turned to exploring feasible elements of witchcraft as they appear in witchcraft trial transcripts and folkloric tales. If we strip away the extreme fantasies related to flying, changing form, devouring infants, and dancing with demons, we can then begin an honest search for the real witch figure. In doing so, we arrive at an enchanted world whose adherents interact with spirits known by many names.

One of the important things we learn is that since ancient times witches have been intimately connected to the plant world. This appears not only in their reliance upon herbs but also in their choice of the wand as a primary tool. It is one of the main implements mentioned in ancient literary works about witches and witchcraft. In chapter four I present witches as "the plant people" and reveal a spiritual tradition behind the connection of herbs, trees, and witches. This chapter also points out the importance of the mandrake, and why crossroads feature so prominently in witchcraft writings. Perhaps most importantly, chapter four expands upon the idea of the Hallow, which is the source through which witches may connect with primal magical energy.

Chapter four also introduces the primary tool of Old Ways witches. This is the mortar and pestle. Through this tool the witch draws upon the forces of the plant realm, not only in the material sense but also in the mystical. One concept that emerges in this chapter is the idea of what is called Shadow. This is a magical force beneath the land that retains the memory of everything absorbed into the earth. This power can be drawn up into plants and made available for use by the witch.

In the last half of the book you will find a witch's grimoire of Old World magic. In this section you will discover uses for the mortar and pestle as the primary tool used by Old Ways witches. The chapter also includes the use of other tools such as the broom and cauldron. Techniques for awakening the "inner witch" are provided along with methods of obtaining familiar spirits and Faery allies. Spells and a variety of symbols also come into play in this section of the book.

Finally, we have the appendices in which I explore the invisible god of witchcraft. In my previous research into deities connected to witchcraft in ancient literature, I never discovered direct mention of a god. There are plenty of ancient references to witches involved with goddesses such as Hecate, Diana, and Proserpina, but the god remained elusive and invisible, if he existed at all. It was through a chance discovery that I encountered a deity who can literally be invisible. He is also directly connected to themes intimately associated with witchcraft. In the final analysis, elements of his depiction in ancient art contributed to the portrayal of demons in the imagery of the Middle Ages and beyond. One very interesting discovery is his connection to lore associated with musicians who go to the crossroads in hopes of trading for heightened musical talent.

The underlying message in this book, as it relates to mainstream and academic views of witchcraft, is simple. Torture, intimidation, and coercion are unreliable methods of producing information for ethnographical studies about witchcraft. We cannot understand what someone believes or practices when we force that person to explain it in terms that conform to what we already believe about them (or what we want to believe).

Additionally, we cannot understand someone's reality when we direct questions toward her or him that are based upon conclusions that preexist in our minds. To do so is not an investigation; it is a manipulation designed to help us arrive at our already expected conclusions. Unfortunately, this approach generated the data that scholars now use to paint a portrait of the history of witches and witchcraft.

It is the intention of this book to have us take a fresh look at the idea of "history" as it applies to witches and witchcraft. It calls for much by way of setting aside our crafted beliefs, at least temporarily, so that we can hear without the *earplugs* of our sense of *personal correctness* stuffed into our ears. To that end I offer the chapters that follow.

Chapter One

HUSHED VOICES
OF THE PAST

This chapter may at first appear to be an argument for witch-craft as the survival of an ancient sect. It is not. Instead it is a look at the evolution of themes related to the witch and witch-craft, which include religious elements and other enduring facets persisting over the centuries. But more than anything else, this chapter is a call to rethink what we believe is the story of witch-craft and to reconsider what we have been led to believe in a different light.

If we listen closely, and with new ears, we can hear the muffled voices of the past speaking to us about witches and witchcraft. These voices seem drowned out by the literary ones of the pre-Christian era and by those of theologians over the centuries of domination by Christian culture in Europe. The witch figure has long been vilified and redefined to fit the personal agenda of the writers in any given period of time. This took place on such a wide scale that we cannot be certain the original witch figure is truly the same unchanged character appearing throughout the centuries.

Scholars freely admit there are problems defining European witchcraft. Several things contribute confusion to this matter including attempts to sort witches from sorceresses and other magic-users. Another problem arises in trying to separate the legendary witch from the human witch, and the reality of witchcraft from its supernatural contamination. Added to this is the mire of learned tradition mixed with popular tradition and vice versa. In other words, how much did the views of theologians and the uneducated people influence one another? Did this influence lead to enlightenment or to conflation and invention?

As mentioned in the preface, I do not believe we possess a documented history of witchcraft. In other words, the academic writings are not an ethnographical study of a people known as witches. What we primarily have instead are writings about the views non-witches held about witchcraft and its practitioners. What is presented as "official history" appears to be largely the examination of how popular beliefs about supernatural beings evolved into an imaginary sect of people. The vast majority of people interrogated on the charge of witchcraft were not witches by any definition. But their coerced confessions to practices they were never a part of contain data scholars use to create a portrait of witchcraft and witches. Can we realistically treat this data as the authentic history of people known as witches?

The modern academic view of witchcraft is rooted in the stereotypes depicted in the writings and records generated by people who feared and hated witches. These roots go much deeper than the Christian era and can be found in ancient Greek and Roman times. The dangerous witch figure is a very old concept. Can such negative views be trusted? How credible are the sources?

Stories about witches have always been quite fantastic and unbelievable. Nevertheless, in previous time periods, people certainly believed in the fantastic. For them it was a real concept that witches flew through the night sky, transformed into various creatures, and frolicked with demons at grand festive celebrations. Such views do not truly match the earliest concepts from which the witch figure evolved. To find the preexisting concepts, we must look to the sparse fragments of the distant past.

What do the earliest writings in Western culture tell us about witches and witchcraft? Despite the modern stereotype of the ugly evil witch, it will surprise the average person to learn of a different depiction in ancient times. There are two sources to examine for a better understanding of the older model of the witch. I refer to ancient literature and etymology, which is the study of the origins of word meanings and how they can change over time or with usage.

In Western culture the earliest word translated into the English word "witch" is the Greek word *pharmakuete* or *pharmakis*. This is also the root of the English word *pharmacist*. The Greek word obviously refers to plants and their chemical properties, but in ancient times it also referred to a particular type of person. Scholar Richard Gordon has commented that pharmakis became one of the standard words for wise woman/witch.[2] What does this suggest about the early nature of witches?

If we look first at the etymology of pharmakis by itself, the image of witches as "the plant people" easily arises. In this light, witches possess knowledge about plants and the effects their substances can create. Having such knowledge is not, by itself, a good or bad thing. It is the application of such knowledge that can be labeled as positive or negative. Popular stories about witches contain references to them healing and harming people. In this light there is no single nature of the witch, and yet in mainstream culture the witch is always thought of as up to no good.

Historically speaking, we know that witches have long been depicted as people of ill intent. In addition, the stereotypes portray the witch as old and ugly. But this image was not always the case. We know, for example, that Medea (a famous witch in ancient literature) first appears as a beautiful woman highly skilled in the arts of witchcraft. She also is portrayed as a priestess of the goddess Hecate.

Another figure is the beautiful Circe, who seduces the Greek hero Ulysses/Odysseus.[3] It is not until the last two centuries before the Christian era that this basic model is transformed and the witch is described as hideous. The writings of the Roman poet Horace appear to be among the earliest to present such a model (and date to the first century before the Christian era). Scholar Richard Gordon states that no extended portraits of hag witches come from the Hellenistic period, although some witches are described as old women in a percentage of tales.[4]

In ancient Greek legends the witch figure appears to be traceable to mythical women known as the Graeae or Graiae. These women first appear in the writings of Hesiod in a work titled *The Theogony*, which dates to around 700 BCE. Hesiod is important because he was the first in Southern Europe to set oral traditions into writing. His writings therefore convey prehistoric concepts. One example is the tale of the Titans, which Hesiod says is so ancient that few people remember anything about the Titans in his own time period.

In *The Theogony*, Hesiod writes that the "Graeae" (commonly written later on as the Graiae) are three sisters born with gray hair, which means they already possess great wisdom at birth. He describes them as fair of face and well clothed. However, in later centuries the Graiae are depicted in the tale of Perseus as three hideous toothless hags who are blind. They possess a magical eye that is passed around in order for all three to share the surrounding view. This is a far cry from the wise and lovely Graiae sisters in Hesiod's earlier period. It is, however, a very good demonstration of how concepts become distorted over time. Later in this chapter we will look at why it takes place.

So far we have explored the etymology in which we encountered the witch as a skilled herbalist or plant specialist. Next we will look at the practice of witchcraft, and from there we will examine the reported character of the witch. This helps us to separate the person of the witch from the legend of the witch. For this task we must first look to the ancient literary works in which witches appear. One of the problems we encounter is the definition of a witch, and whether or not the translation from one language to another should rightfully read "witch" (as opposed to someone who uses magic in general). In other words, is the character really a witch as opposed to a sorceress? Is there a difference?

The majority of the earliest tales of witches are actually fictitious. For this reason, there is a tendency in the academic field to dismiss the material as any kind of proof about authentic practices of witches and witchcraft in ancient times. However, a good fiction typically contains true elements along with invented ones. For example, a piece of fiction written about a gang in Chicago will incorporate real places, known slang, and current popular beliefs about gang members. This helps the reader relate better to the story itself because it seems more believable due to the familiar components. I view ancient fiction in the same way. I do not regard the ancient literary tales as historical accounts, but I do believe they contain historical elements. In this sense there is a "folklore as history" component here, and we should not automatically dismiss its value.

One featured element in the earliest tales of witches is the calling upon of stars in the night sky. A woman referred to as Giula of Bologna was accused of witchcraft (circa 1518) and condemned by the Inquisition for praying to a star called Diana. Scholar Matteo Duni comments on the appearance in witchcraft trials of such non-Christian elements as praying to the stars and the moon.[5] This type of thing is very old magic, and evoking the aid of stars is a known historical practice of great antiquity. Among the earliest examples are evocations found in ancient Chaldea or Babylon. The extreme closeness between these historical verses and the witchcraft evocations appearing in ancient Greek and Roman literature is remarkable. Is this coincidence, or are we looking at something more significant?

Tales about the witch figure known as Medea are rich with old magic and contain the evocation of stars. Medea uses a wand, a knife, a cauldron, and an altar. These are the earliest referenced tools used by a witch. She works her witchcraft primarily at night and calls not only upon the stars but also on very primal forces. These include mountains, rivers, lakes, forests, and herbs.[6] The idea that inanimate objects possess consciousness and power is extremely ancient. Additionally, Medea calls upon goddesses such as Hecate. This, coupled with the use of an altar, suggests a religious or spiritual connection. Indeed, in ancient tales Medea is described as a priestess.

Modern scholars reject the view of witchcraft as a religion in the past. Despite such a position, no historical era is without a religious connotation regarding witches and witchcraft. For example, in the Middle Ages and Renaissance witches were believed to "worship" the Devil. But scholars do not regard this element as something religious in nature, which is a curious position to maintain.[7] It is interesting to note that in ancient Greek culture witches are described as practitioners of *illicit religion*, which means their practices were not regarded as meeting the standards of official religion as set forth by the authorities. No matter how much the practices of a witch looked religious in nature, witches were never granted that status by those sitting in judgment of such things.

In ancient times the people of all regions were exposed to the idea of gods and goddesses. Records indicate a widespread veneration of deities in all social classes. The witches of ancient culture grew up in the same world of non-witches. It is unlikely that they alone were unaware of the gods, uninterested, or completely uninvolved. Were ancient witches entirely uninfluenced by the regional cultures in which they lived? This seems very unlikely, and so we must take into consideration that ancient witches had some type of relationship with the gods.

When examining ancient literature associated with witches and witchcraft we encounter a complex problem. Historically, and in the literary tradition, witches have always been depicted as evil, dangerous, self-serving, and ill-intentioned people, but it is not uncommon for the enemy to always be viewed in such a light; therefore, everything they do is interpreted in accord with the preconception. We see this practice reflected in the attitudes related to the American Indian wars. When Indians were triumphant in battle, it is called a massacre, whereas defeat by the U.S. Army is a victory. It is really a matter of who is telling the story and what they have to gain. The bad guys are always the people belonging to the other side.

It is not my intent to portray ancient witches as a loving but misunderstood people. There were certainly sound reasons to fear witches in days of old, just as there were good reasons to fear any powerful people treated badly in ancient times. Jason (of Argonaut fame) manipulates the love Medea has for him as a means of getting her to use magic to achieve his goals through ill deeds. Afterward he leaves her and their children and runs off to marry another woman. But he remains the noble Greek hero, and she is the villain. In the mythical story of Ulysses/Odysseus, he has an affair with Circe and leaves her behind to return to his wife after one year's time. In the tale he is the good guy and she is the bad girl.[8]

The most common stories about witches have them using poison and evoking foul weather in their preferred enjoyment of making life miserable for others. In the records of old witch trials we read accounts that witches are required to report their ill deeds to the Devil on a regular basis. We are further told that witches are beaten for poor performance and insufficient evil acts. That this type of nonsense was ever regarded as fact is even more unbelievable than the allegations made against witches.

We know from anthropological studies that the witch figure was a tool used to explain bad times, illness, and harmful acts of nature. Sick cattle, poor crops, unexplainable illness, negative weather changes, and odd phenomena were all attributed to the presence and activities of a witch. Kill the witch, fix the problem. Therefore, the legendary evil witch filled a needed place, which was that of the scapegoat.

It is one of the goals of this book to demonstrate that actual people existed who were witches. These were not the legendary or supernatural witches. Instead they were mortals like any, but mortals who possessed what can be called "an enchanted view" of the world around them. I refer to these people as Old Ways witches. They were the lineage bearers of the old magic and old practices that were disappearing under the pressure of the Church to eradicate pre-Christian beliefs and practices. These witches were not inherently evil, but they were more than capable and willing to harm their enemies as deemed necessary.

According to historian Richard Gordon, in ancient times there were two types of witches. One was the kind that could be encountered in daily life, and who was known about in her community. The other type was the supernatural or "night witch"—an impossible creature that was a vampire-like owl who could transform into a woman.[9] The latter overshadowed the mortal witch and gave rise to displaced fear and violent persecution. Ironically, the blending of the real witch with the imaginary one eventually produced a positive result. This was the disbelief in the existence of witches in the past or the present. Time fused the two types of witches into one in the public mind. The eventual realization that the supernatural witch was a false concept automatically dismissed the idea of the existence of the witch itself. It was safer for witches to have people not believe in them, and so both sides shared the relief of disbelief when its time came.

One key problem in ferreting out the Old Ways witch is that the old stories about witches are all about the supernatural witch, and many of the folk customs still carry a belief in her. By comparison it is rare to find ancient tales of the mortal witch, and as a result some people conclude there weren't any. This erroneous assessment much too easily misleads people and directs them away from pursuing the buried truth. Finding the truth about ancient witches requires removing the coverings of distortion, intentional misrepresentation, political fabrication, and the invention of diabolical witchcraft by the Church and its agents.

In order to arrive at an understanding of witchcraft as it once was, as opposed to its misrepresentation, we must use the basic science of *reverse engineering*. Essentially, this science attempts to acquire knowledge about the original model or mechanism of something when little or nothing is known about it. The process starts with examining the model as it currently exists and then working backward through its connective parts. The trail is followed by examining the sequence of the parts, how they are assembled, and the function each plays, all the way back to the first part of the original model. By doing so, it is possible to come to a realization of the original idea or its generative form.

In relationship to witchcraft, we need to apply reverse engineering to popular folklore and diabolical witchcraft as well as to the views of the Church and its agents in the past. This is the story of how old witchcraft traditions were suppressed or demonized. It is also the tale of how popular beliefs and customs can be cultivated to displace or distort the cultural roots of their origin. Uncovering that origin is a worthy quest.

The work ahead of us begins with the idea of the diabolical witch and the stereotype of the Sabbat as a blasphemy against the Catholic mass. An examination of its invented components and the tracing back in time of its non-diabolical roots will begin to unravel the hoax. Investigating each of the elements helps to follow the ideas about witches and witchcraft that were grafted onto the theme, each one forming links in a forged chain of falsehoods.

Aside from the evil nature of the witch figure in mainstream society, the pre-Christian depiction of the witch is different in key ways. Over time the witch was transformed from a sorceress calling upon a goddess of witchcraft to a deviant worshipping the Devil. The latter obliterated the earlier model and fixed the public mind on a new enemy of Christian society. The fictional witch of pre-Christian literary tradition was thereby reshaped into the fictional witch of popular Christian culture. This was reinforced with transplanted ideas about witches and witchcraft from theologians and other agents of the Church.

The Christianized image of the witch is a cultivated one. It came along hand in hand with the vilification of pre-Christian deities, practices, and beliefs that were contrary to the theology of Christianity. With the resources of the Church, and a multitude of individuals devoted to converting pagans, the culture and spirit of the pre-Christian European people were beaten into submission. The campaign is what I refer to as spiritual ethnocide, which targeted not only beliefs and practices but also the enchanted worldview of paganism and its adherents. The witch, as she or he was once known, became one of the many casualties.

Duni describes the fourteenth-century trial of two women named Sibilla Zanni and Pierina Bugatis. They reportedly confessed to attending the night assembly presided over by Madonna Oriente/Diana. Duni refers to elements within the women's confession that reflect pre-Christian rituals associated with goddesses of abundance.[10] He goes on to say the judges concluded that the women were deceived into believing the entity they venerated was a goddess, and that in fact it could only be the Devil in disguise. The women's voices are hushed, the goddess is dismissed, and the Devil takes the field.

The use of art was also influential in transforming pre-Christian deity forms into the Devil. Historian Jeffrey Russell notes that in medieval art the image of a demon contains a composite of attributes previously belonging to ancient Greek deities. One example he provides is that demons are depicted with traces of the wings of Hermes Psychopompos on their legs. The shape of their bodies is based upon those of Pan and Dionysos, and they bear the facial structure of Charun (an Underworld entity with a beaked nose).[11] The Bible does not contain physical descriptions of demons or of the Devil. Since there are no illustrations derived directly from biblical text, what then is the purpose of using pre-Christian imagery in such an unrelated and distorted fashion?

Spiritual Ethnocide and the Dominance of Popular Folk Traditions

In this section we will look at the idea that the Church, through its agents, intentionally altered ideas about pre-Christian beliefs and practices. In some cases new ideas were entirely invented. The goal was to discourage people from continuing to practice traditions that were in conflict with Christian culture. This was put into motion by banning certain practices and adopting others in a modified form better suited to the Church's position. Underlying it all was the message that pre-Christian ways led to spiritual damnation and the Christian path led to spiritual salvation.

There is no question that pre-Christian ways continued through the centuries. We have ample evidence in the form of admonishments that appear in sermons and laws enacted to outlaw a variety of practices. It is also clear that where such beliefs and practices could not be stamped out they were Christianized and allowed within the new form of celebration. Some people call such elements a survival of paganism. Others argue that they do not constitute paganism because the people embracing them are not pagans. Therefore, in accord with such a view, paganism itself did not survive.

The term "survival" is problematic when discussing traces of pagan or witchcraft elements in the traditions of Christian culture. One of the problems is that it can mean something different among Neo-Pagans than it does within the academic community. The truth of the matter can only be discerned by comprehending what "continues" into a new culture versus what is "adapted" or "adopted" by it (and for what purpose).

In mainstream culture, customs frequently change and adapt to fit new ideas. If these ideas are popular, there is little resistance to the change; when resistance does exist, it is often not significant enough to derail the movement. No one in authority holds popular culture by the reins through established checks and balances. By contrast, the underground or outcast society does consciously try to retain its ways despite the lure of the latest fad appearing in society. After all, the subculture is all about having and maintaining an identity that separates it from mainstream culture.

When we look at folk customs and folk magic practices in the Christian era, we see two things. First, we can note fragments of pre-Christian pagan practices, and second, we observe the appearance of relatively new customs. One example of a pagan practice in Christian usage appears in the festival of St. Dominic in the village of Cocullo, Italy (in the region of Abruzzo). On the first Thursday of May, St. Dominic's statue is carried on a platform through the streets and is covered with living snakes. As the statue passes by, people attach their petitions to it for special requests. The village of Cocullo was formerly the pre-Christian worship site of the serpent goddess known as Angizia, who was venerated in the same fashion in her time as is St. Dominic today.

In the currently existing European folk magic traditions of Christian culture, we find a variety of herbs. Each has a specific power attributed to it because it reportedly grew at the foot of the cross in the tale of the death of Jesus. The problem is that all the ascribed herbs could not possibly have grown in the climate and conditions of the region. So the fact that power is attributed to these herbs almost certainly comes from a preexisting assignment to the source of magical properties. The base of this power must have been rooted in pre-Christian European culture. Therefore, what we have here is the arrogation of the magical herbal tradition from non-Christian sources, and one that displaced the pagan system and its magical connections. It is because of this devious practice that I feel modern folk culture has intentionally suppressed the truth about its magical roots. This suppression resulted in regarding the relatively new traditions and customs as being the original ones. The problem with this view is that it creates the false impression that the declared existence of earlier forms and uses is an invention by Neo-Pagans and others.

Next we need to look at the question of whether or not previous pagan traditions continued despite their encounter with Christian culture. There is widespread disagreement about the idea of the survival of pre-Christian traditions. Some people believe that all elements of paganism in Europe were completely eradicated by Christianity. Others believe that pagan customs were absorbed by Christianity and completely transformed into Christian traditions where they ceased being pagan in nature. The rarest of all beliefs is that some pagan and witchcraft traditions survived and continued as non-Christian practices into modern times.

Scholar Bernadette Filotas has commented on the weakness of relying upon various sources from which academic conclusions are derived. In particular, she points to the early Middle Ages and notes that except for Roman religion, there is sparse information about those pagan rituals and beliefs that left no archaeological traces and for which the only source is the writings of Christian clerics.[12] This is interesting because it demonstrates a weakness in archaeological studies but also because it points to relying upon Christian clerics to provide an accurate depiction and understanding of a rival faith—paganism. This seems unlikely at best.

The story of witchcraft stands at a crossroads where conflict marks the center. On one branch we have what can be called the "learned" or hegemonic view. On the other is what is sometimes referred to as "subaltern" culture. This term denotes the suppressed beliefs and practices of peasant culture that are ignored or denied by an exclusive focus on academically recognized studies of popular culture. Rather than realizing the perspective held by each, the reaction is typically to see one as falsehood and the other as truth.

Sicilian folklorist Giuseppe Pitrè once commented that "The significant history of a people, not to be confused with the history of their rulers, is to be found in folkloric beliefs and customs transmitted orally or enacted in rituals."[13] I believe there is truth in this statement, but this truth is only partial because folkloric beliefs shift and are modified over time. It is easy to conclude that the surviving commonalities found in folkloric beliefs must be the most profound, and thus have the deepest roots. But this is not always the case. On occasion it is the small fragments that reside in the backdrop of folk beliefs and practices that are foundational in nature. These elements echo back to the distant past long before the One God came to displace the Many. This will become apparent in the following chapters.

The conversion of pagans to Christianity was a planned project and not a natural process of spiritual evolution. In my opinion, it constitutes a war of spiritual ethnocide against the indigenous population of Europe and their beliefs and practices. The Church set out to intentionally demonize and vilify pre-Christian ways. In doing so, it suppressed as well as eradicated many older beliefs and practices (and assimilated others in an attempt to de-*paganize* them). In addition, the practice of torture and execution was put into use in hopes of stamping out resistance as well as ensuring a strict adherence to Christianity. This is cultural violence both figuratively and literally.

One of the less obvious means of stamping out pre-Christian beliefs and practices was to change their purpose. This allowed people the continued familiarity of ancestral ways while at the same time transforming them with a Christianized theme. In time, the pre-Christian roots were forgotten as the proceeding generational experience became purely Christian in nature. The old pagans had long since died and were replaced by generations of people who were raised in a Christian Europe. But was anything ever truly forgotten?

In an ironic sense, it was the Catholic Church itself that helped preserve former pagan practices. This is not only in terms of adapting them to conform to Christian practices but also through the writings of the Church and its agents. It is here that we find admonishments against pre-Christian practices, which reveal what these practices were as well as their popularity. This record allows us to look into the past to authenticate pre-Christian practices through comparison with writings from past periods. It also allows us to look forward into the centuries that follow the Church's early admonishments. In this way, we can trace the persistence of pre-Christian elements even where they become absorbed and reworked into something Christian. We will examine this further in forthcoming chapters.

Another factor that we need to understand is the role of popular folklore and folk traditions. These also fall under the heading of popular belief and popular culture. As such, it is regarded by academics as the empirical truth. The problem is that what it truly reflects is the domination of one thing over another. In other words, it is what prevails and thereby displaces what came before it. The latter is the subaltern or submerged culture that is suppressed by hegemonic society. One very strong example is that of the Black Madonna in Catholic culture and the figure of a pre-Christian goddess who was still venerated well into the Christian era. The dominating view of the Black Madonna is that this is a representation of the "Mother of God" in Catholicism and is not connected to a pre-Christian goddess. The view of the suppressed culture is that the Black Madonna displaces the ancient goddess from which she originated and disassociates herself from paganism. She is the goddess turned saint who no longer acknowledges her past and who changes her identity to invent a new persona in a new community.

It is worth noting that the ancient Greek writer known as Pausanias mentions in his work titled *Description of Greece* (10. 36. 5) an Artemis/Diana figure made of black stone. In the archaeological museum of Naples resides the ancient statue of a black Artemis/Diana of Ephesus that is nearly seven feet tall. This goddess is a mother figure decorated with multiple animals and having multiple breasts with which to feed them. It was at Ephesus, the city where Artemis-Diana was venerated, that the church proclaimed St. Mary as the "Mother of God" in 431 CE. Is the emphasis of St. Mary as "mother" a mere coincidence in this city of the ancient Mother Goddess, or is this something contrived to displace one by the other?

Divine feminine figures and cave drawings discovered near Palermo date 30,000 years before the Christian era. Others are found on the islands of Malta and Sardinia, and date from 6,000 to 3,500 years before the Christian era. What they have in common are two things. First, they appear to represent a mother goddess concept, and second, they were discovered in the Paleolithic and Neolithic sites that later became the sanctuaries of the Black Madonna statuary. We find an excellent examination of this subject in historian Lucia Chiavola Birnbaum's *Black Madonnas*.[14]

It appears clear enough that the Black Madonna is a Christian adaptation of a pagan deity modified for use in Christian culture, but most scholars reject the abundance of evidence as being nothing more than coincidence. This strange logic applies not only to themes of deities, but also arises in folk magic traditions and is specifically related to symbolic charms in such systems. One such charm is the *cimaruta*, which in popular tradition is an Italian amulet intended to provide protection from malevolent enchantments. The charm is designed in the fashion of a sprig of the herb known as rue. A variety of symbolic charms is attached to the ends of the rue plant design.

Most of what is publicly known about the cimaruta comes from the late nineteenth-century writings of folklorists. It is referred to as a charm against such things as "evil" and black magic in general. The majority of old references inform us that the cimaruta was hung on the crib of a newborn infant. Its purpose here was to deflect the envy of visitors, an act that could cast the evil eye and harm the infant. This charm is one of many used by superstitious Catholics in Italy during the nineteenth century, but when we examine the symbolism of the cimaruta, it becomes difficult to understand how it meshes with Catholic beliefs in such a way that the charm reflects Christian tenets. We should expect to find Christian symbolism in a charm designed to protect Catholics, but in its earliest forms, such symbols are not truly represented on the cimaruta.

The nineteenth-century cimaruta charm was most commonly comprised of several symbols that readily identified it. These were attached to the sprig of rue design, encircling it to form one complete amulet. All cimaruta pieces of this era contained the following symbols.

1. Hand
2. Moon
3. Key
4. Flower
5. Horn or dagger
6. Rooster (or sometimes an eagle)
7. Serpent

Later other symbols were added to the cimaruta. Among the most common were the heart, the cornucopia, and the cherub angel. The later addition of the heart (sometimes depicted as a flaming heart) and the cherub are the only ones to reflect Catholic theology. When we compare this cimaruta design with earlier ones, the heart or the cherub is always placed on areas that are empty spaces in the older designs. What does that suggest?

When first introduced to the cimaruta, I was informed that it is a witch's charm. In the past, witches reportedly wore it as a sign of their secret society. Since that time, I have encountered the belief that the cimaruta is an anti-witchcraft charm. I believe this erroneous assessment is due to the ancient reputation of the rue plant as a protection against sorcery and poisoning. Unfortunately, any word used to denote sorcery is often translated into the word witch or witchcraft. This makes it difficult to know precisely what was intended in the original references. In other words, was the word "witch" inserted to replace sorceress or wizard? Some people make no distinction between a user of magic and a witch, but one goal of this book is to demonstrate the true difference.

Upon examining the symbols on the cimaruta, we find that, with the exception of the added heart and angel, all of them were used as pre-Christian symbols. Each of the common symbols on the cimaruta is associated with the practice of witchcraft as opposed to its prevention. If the cimaruta is a charm against witchcraft, then it is an ineffective one in terms of its expressed symbolism. When we look at it as the witch's charm, however, the symbolism makes complete sense. Let us examine each symbol on the cimaruta.

The human hand has long been depicted among the occult symbols of magic. Historian Ruth Martin comments on the use of the hand in witchcraft to cast spells and summon spirits.[15] In palmistry, the fingers of the hand are assigned planetary connections and many magical systems use a variety of ritual hand gestures. In this light, the appearance of the hand on the cimaruta is in keeping with its being a witch's charm. The objection to this might arise when we look at popular folk customs in which we find the *mano cornuto* (horned-hand) and *the mano in fico* (fig-hand). In popular folk tradition, each of these is intended to drive away ill intent, which the superstitious often call witchcraft. But when we consider that in Italian culture these gestures are used against non-witches as well, we must then conclude that these hand symbols are not specifically anti-witchcraft. They are instead gestures of general protection and deflection against unwanted influences in general.

The next symbol we find on the cimaruta is the moon. This symbol requires no argument that it is favorable to witchcraft and witches. What is puzzling is how the moon can be regarded on the cimaruta as an anti-witchcraft symbol. I know of nothing in Catholic theology that could support this idea. We do see images of the Virgin Mary standing on a crescent, which some people may view as the triumph of the new religion over the old (solar versus lunar), but I have never encountered this theme in connection with the crescent moon on the cimaruta. In common folklore, the moon often appears on charms for protection, but no explanation is provided. However, it has been suggested that the horned tips of the crescent render it a protective symbol in general. But how does the symbol of the moon protect a person from a witch, when the witch is someone who works lunar magic?

Next in order is the symbol of the key. The most obvious connection to it as a witch's charm is its association with Hecate, a classic goddess of witchcraft and witches. The key was one of the primary symbols of Hecate in her role as the keeper of thresholds. It appears on her statuary along with a serpent and a torch (some sources replace the serpent with a whip). While it is true that in Catholic tradition, St. Peter is often depicted holding the key to heaven, it seems unlikely that this is the reason for including a key on the cimaruta. If it were, how can control over the door of heaven be a protection against witches on earth? Here again, we find another symbol on the cimaruta that falls short of relevance to Catholic theology in terms of protection from witchcraft. By contrast, the key fits nicely with the symbolic use by witches in the service of Hecate.

The flower on the cimaruta is described as a vervain, lotus, or clover, but its shape on the old cimaruta charms bears little, if any, resemblance to the last two flowers. I was originally taught that the flower is a vervain blossom, and I have yet to find any reason to reject that assignment. Flowers in general, being part of a plant, have no negative effect on witches, who are masters of the plant world. However, various plants and trees have a magical reputation for protection against enchantments. In this context, it may be that the blossom on the cimaruta was meant to convey this idea, and to superstitious people in the nineteenth century this meant protection against witchcraft. However, to the witch, the vervain blossom signifies the alliance with the Faery race, which gives power to the cimaruta as a witch's charm.

We turn now to the horn symbol. The horn has long represented power and virility, and as such does fall into the overall category of protection. In this regard, the concept is well rooted in paganism and less arguable as a Catholic symbol against enchantment; however, the horn is mentioned in the New Testament as a Christian symbol. One example appears in Luke 1:69, which reads *"The Lord has raised up the horn of salvation for us in the house of his servant David."* Another example appears in the Book of Revelation 5:6, which refers to the Lamb of God having seven horns that are the seven spirits of God. Is this the meaning of the horn on the cimaruta? It seems unlikely. By contrast, the horn has significance to the witch through the association of horned goats, a traditional association with witchcraft.

The symbol of the rooster presents a small problem on the cimaruta. This creature is most often associated with sunrise, a time that brings an end to the realm of night where the moon rules supreme. In this regard, we can understand how the rooster can be viewed as an anti-witch symbol. However, the rooster is one of the cult animals of the god Apollo. This deity is the brother of Diana, a goddess associated with witchcraft since ancient times. In this relationship, the sun and moon are not antagonistic toward one another. Therefore, the sun and the rooster need not be viewed as an anti-witchcraft symbol. I was taught that the rooster represents the banisher of illusion, the light dispersing what is imagined in the night. In this way, it relates to the witch as a seer, a person who can dispel falsehoods and see beyond a facade.

The last symbol on the cimaruta is that of the serpent. Like the moon symbol, there is no reason to regard the serpent as an anti-witch charm. In Catholic tradition, the serpent represents the Devil. The inclusion of the serpent as an anti-witchcraft charm on the cimaruta is nonsensical. However, the serpent appears in many writings about witches and witchcraft. Among the most notable connections is the famous witches' walnut tree in Benevento. When the Lombards occupied the city, the walnut tree was the site of serpent veneration. A gold statue of a winged serpent was featured in the celebrations, which included participants circling the serpent with their backs turned toward it. St. Barbatus ordered the tree cut down and had the statue melted and formed into "a sacred paten," which was preserved up to the time of the French invasion in 1799.[16] Other accounts state that the statue was made into a chalice.

The examination of the cimaruta symbolism reveals that there is very little support for it as a protective charm in Catholic culture. The preponderance of evidence shows the symbolism on the cimaruta to be pre-Christian in origin and nature. Overall, the charms on the cimaruta are protective symbols, and indeed one of the uses for it is against enchantments. But even witches use charms against ill-intended magic directed against them. Therefore, the anti-enchantment intent of the cimaruta does not make it a repellent of witches. Clearly, there is much more cause to view the cimaruta as a witch's charm than there is to regard it as an anti-witch device.

The majority of modern folklorists and anthropologists insist that the cimaruta is an anti-witchcraft charm. They base this upon the dominating folk tradition of the period in which writings are found about the cimaruta. This approach ignores the pre-Christian roots of the symbolism in favor of the hegemonic position of the dominating folklore of the nineteenth century. It rejects suppressed culture in favor of ruling culture. This is yet another example of spiritual ethnocide against pre-Christian beliefs and practices.

The displacement of pre-Christian ways is evident in much of contemporary folk magic and religion. Earlier we saw that plants with pre-Christian uses in magic were transformed into Christianized folk magic plants. Each of the plants is attributed a magical nature because it allegedly grew at the foot of the cross, but we know this is false because the climate does not allow all of these plants to survive in the region of Jerusalem. Despite this, the lore of these plants in popular folk tradition now dominates the older traditions and has displaced them. The falsified roots of Christianized magical plants have become the accepted tradition behind the attributes of plants in folk magic as well as their origin.

It is because of invented traditions and imagined roots that I believe much of the spiritual ethnocide against pre-Christian beliefs and practices was intentional, and remains so to this day. This includes treatment of the witch figure. In the next chapter, we will look at the evolution of the witch figure over centuries. In doing so, we will uncover more evidence of deception and invention throughout the Christian era. Through this we will discover the witch as part of a submerged and repressed culture dominated and displaced by popular beliefs of hegemonic society.

Chapter Two

CONCOCTING A WITCH

The idea of witchcraft as an ancient sect that survived through the centuries is often called a Neo-Pagan fabrication. In kinder terms, it is sometimes referred to as the romantic notion of the witch and witchcraft. Be that as it may, the academic depiction of the witch figure is absolutely an invented one. Here we are devoted to examining the "official" portrait of witches and witch-craft. In doing so, we will see how the witch figure evolved and how theologians helped to distort the end results.

The stereotypical European witch figure is frequently depicted as someone who uses magic for negative purposes, is diabolical in nature, worships the Devil, is cannibalistic, and participates in depraved acts and sexual perversion. This image of the witch is a compilation of individual ideas mixed together to create a single portrait. While it is true that the witch has always been portrayed in an unfavorable light, there was certainly a time when the Judeo-Christian Devil was not part of the picture. The Devil is an addition to the idea of witchcraft, and the association comes many centuries after the rise of Christianity.

The definition of the witch as a person venerating the Devil does not appear in pre-Christian writings about witches and witchcraft. Instead the ancient Greek and Roman literature includes references to witches involved with such goddesses as Hecate, Diana, and Proserpina. In the Christian era, the connection of the witch to a powerful being is reworked to conform to a different worldview related to the Devil. It should be noted here that the Devil is not linked with witches until the Middle Ages.

In reality, if there were people venerating the Devil and performing the kinds of acts reported in European witchcraft trials, why are they not called Satanists or devil-worshippers instead of witches? After all, the preexisting tales of witches always associated them with goddesses. This literary tradition spans almost a thousand years from the time of the ancient Greek and Roman writings into the Christian era. Dismissal of the basic concept is rejected by Church doctrine in the tenth-century text known as the Canon Episcopi. If "witches" were worshipping the Devil in the Christian era, how did this go unaddressed by the Church for more than 900 years? As we will see in this chapter, the Devil is not introduced into witchcraft until many centuries after the rise of Christianity.

In order to uncover the Old World witch as she or he was, versus the imagined one of popular belief, we must first deconstruct the stereotype. The contemporary image of the witch is a toothless hag with green skin and warts on her nose and chin. As previously noted, in earlier periods the witch is portrayed as a diabolical character worshipping the Devil, eating infants, and harming people, animals, and crops. Long before that, she was a beautiful and powerful sorceress in ancient Greek tales. It seems that the years have not been kind to the witch.

As noted in chapter one, it is important to understand that the official academic view of European witchcraft does not come from a cultural study of people calling themselves witches. We touched on the idea earlier that what is presented as "the history of witchcraft" is instead a chronology of superstitions and legends and how they developed to form beliefs about people who were labeled witches. This process took centuries to ripen, and it was cemented by the introduction into folk tradition of various "authoritative" writings and commentaries. The bulk of this comprises sermons, chronicles, judicial manuals, pamphlets, and various treatises on witchcraft (as promoted by the learned class). In the final analysis, the popular and academic depiction of European witches and witchcraft is the end result of centuries of invention and conflation.

It is important to be aware of the difference between folk tradition (popular beliefs of the people) and the learned tradition (beliefs of the educated class). Folk tradition reflects the beliefs, lore, and superstition of a people (even though this lore can and does change over time). The learned tradition, in the case of witchcraft, represents the views of judges, interrogators, theologians, commentators, and official Church doctrine. There came a time when contamination occurred as the inevitable merging of the two took place. In other words, the people were continually exposed to learned ideas that influenced their beliefs. This exposure most likely took place through witch trials, sermons, and spoken condemnations at public executions. In addition, the circulating of pamphlets and public notices no doubt introduced official views into the populace. On the other side, learned tradition was influenced by popular beliefs among the people of any given period. This is evident in the fact that the writings of the educated class address the popular period beliefs in which they appear and use them to support and justify the application of laws, edicts, rulings, and judgments.

Historians argue among themselves concerning their view of what they define as witchcraft (a perspective I call *"academic-viewed witchcraft"* as opposed to *Old World witchcraft*). Some scholars believe the essential ideas of academic-viewed witchcraft are derived from popular tradition. Others feel that the origin is rooted in ideas inserted by the learned class of theologians and inquisitors. Another school of thought holds that ideas about witchcraft were formed from actual diabolical practices, but this position belongs to a weakening group of scholars.

Anthropologists expand the definition of witchcraft beyond Europe to include African and American Indian cultures as well as others. Their definition of witchcraft focuses on black magic or any form intended to cause harm. Therefore, any magic-user who performs a harmful act through magic is a witch. From an anthropological perspective, the difference between a sorceress and a witch is that the witch possesses the ability to influence by pure thought, will, or mere presence. By contrast, a sorceress requires a ritual or magical procedure.

Anthropologists study the culture of a people, their customs, lore, social structure, and basic beliefs and practices. While this can tell us much about popular traditions and mainstream beliefs, the study can also fall short of rooting out and understanding the foundational traditions of the submerged or subaltern culture. The prevailing popular traditions dominate the suppressed ones that were displaced over time. Another problem is that, when considering European witchcraft, the data contained in confessions produced by torture can hardly be relied upon as reflective of true cultural beliefs and practices. Instead it largely reflects what the inquisitors wanted to hear. Therefore, the most we can glean from these reports is an understanding of the culture of non-witches and their views about a people (witches) that largely existed only in their imagination.

Historian Richard Kieckhefer points out that some scholars such as Joseph Hansen and Rossell H. Robbins note clear distinctions between elements of learned tradition versus popular belief.[17] These historians conclude that such elements of witchcraft as supernatural flight, physical transformation, and diabolical assemblies are not derived from popular beliefs or practices. Instead these are concepts invented by medieval theologians drawing upon Christian and Greco-Roman traditions. However, Kieckhefer adds that Jacob Grimm felt the portrayal of witchcraft was influenced by Germanic folklore, which does imply popular belief.

When we speak of popular beliefs about witchcraft, we are considering the cultural views of a people about a topic, which is not necessarily reflective of the ultimate truth. Ideas held by the majority about minorities are those of outsiders, which is very problematic. The same can be said of theologians, judges, and inquisitors who operated during the centuries of the witch trials. To further confuse the issue, the word "witch" was widely applied to anyone performing magic. At times this even included the Cunning Folk, a sect of folk magic practitioners who were adamant about not being witches. This contaminates the data used to arrive at an accurate academic definition of the witch.

For an understanding of the witch figure, it will help to start at the beginning and follow the twisted trail. The story begins with witches as people intent on harm and causing it whenever possible. This theme appears in the pre-Christian era as well as the Christian period. The actions of harmful witches are never truly examined from the witches' perspective; they are simply regarded as hand in hand with the ever-present evil nature of the witch. This theme never changes over the centuries, and it actually becomes amplified in the depiction of the diabolical witch of the Middle Ages and Renaissance. To understand the roots of such a concept in Western culture, we must look to ancient ideas about magic.

One popular view is that the Persians introduced magic into ancient Greece; or at least ideas about magic among the Greeks come from Persian influences. Occult techniques known among Babylonians, Assyrians, and Persians appear to reach Greece and Italy in their prehistory. During the Hellenistic period, other influences are introduced from Egypt. The often hostile relationship between Greece and Persia caused a negative view of magic in Western culture, and its practitioners were therefore not to be trusted with good intentions.

Over the course of time, ideas about magic-users merged with popular beliefs of the culture. Archaic beliefs about supernatural beings and the appearance of magic-users in the culture became a formula for conflation. Eventually, the two ideas morphed into one—the witch. In Southern Europe we 'find the ancient creature know as a *strix* or a *striga*. This creature was a vampire-like being that took the form of a hideous owl and could also appear as an old woman. The merging of the strix/striges with the witch figure appears in various ancient works by such writers as Ovid. He often describes the striges as ravenous birds with hooked beaks and powerful talons. They have gray feathers and a large head with peering eyes. Ovid notes the belief in them being able to transform into human shape. The Roman poet Horace (first century BCE) openly mocks the idea of such a concept in his work titled *Ars Poetica* (verses 338–40). His writings about witches depict them as fully human (as evidenced in his work known as the *Epodes*), but during the following first two centuries of the Christian era, we find an abundance of references to striges as though such creatures were real.

The strix/striga is the root of the mythical witch in Southern European tradition but later influences ideas about witches in Northern Europe. This takes place due to the translation of Greek and Latin material about witches which is eventually used by the authorities in other regions of Europe. Later in this chapter, we will examine ideas about witches in Britain, Germany, and Eastern Europe.

The grammarian known as Sextus Pompeius Festus (first century CE) defined the Latin word *strigae* as "*the name given to women who practice sorcery, and who are also called flying women.*"[18] This is revealing in terms of noting the existence of a mortal witch figure and the related belief in its supernatural counterpart. As we saw in chapter one, historian Richard Gordon makes a distinction between the supernatural night-witch and the human-witch in ancient times. He notes that no one ever saw a *night-witch* but people could encounter the mortal witch in daily life.

Historian Norman Cohn remarks that most ancient writers knew perfectly well that the striges or strigae were completely imaginary. He also notes that writers of the period used the idea of such creatures to "ornament" their writings about witches.[19] However, Cohn also comments that ancient literary references reflect a "serious belief" in the strix/striges that may have been widespread among the common people. Historian Richard Gordon remarks that "*tensions and interactions*" existed between the peasant class and the educated class related to the development of magical beliefs.[20] Scholar Ronald Hutton once noted the lament of ancient philosophers who were dismayed that the uneducated maintained their beliefs despite exposure to the orations of the learned class.[21]

The primary depiction in the early tradition of witches as evil comes largely from such ancient poets as Theocritus, Vergil, Horace, Seneca, and Lucan (and we have already noted the writer Ovid). From such sources, we see reflections of the vernacular traditions of witchcraft as known throughout the Roman Empire. If we peel away the politics and agenda of the writers, and set aside for a moment the depicted evil nature of the witch, we can examine some important background information. It is here that we can encounter the workings of the mortal witch.

From an examination of the ancient literature about witches, we find the following elements as persistent themes. Witches call upon celestial forces (stars and moon), use herbs and ritual tools (wand, knife, and cauldron), and make images of people from wax or some other substance for magical purposes. They also evoke or call upon a goddess (most frequently Hecate or Diana). In their portrayal, witches do not possess magical power from within; in other words, they are not internally magical. In order to perform a work of magic, the witch must use tools and a process such as a ritual or some means of casting a spell. They have access to power but do not self-generate power. If we stay with this relatively reasonable theme and avoid the fantastic elements of the supernatural, we can better dismantle the distorted image of the invented witch.

Returning to the idea of the striges or night-witches, the concept surfaces outside of Southern Europe where it is documented in the sixth century of the Christian era. The earliest body of German law—the *Lex Salica*—reflects old beliefs of previous times. It treats the "stria," or "striga," as a reality, and includes the cannibalistic nature of the creature that also appears in ancient Roman literature.[22] It is noteworthy that these German beliefs exist prior to influences by the Romans or the Christians. This suggests a widespread belief among the common people in a similar if not identical type of supernatural being. Perhaps it is not too surprising that this figure becomes the witch in many regions of Europe. We must bear in mind, however, that this is not the witch we are looking for in this book; it is instead a conflation of a mythical creature with a specific type of human being.

The pattern of inventing a witch continues through the centuries, and another element seems to surface in the early tenth century. It is here that we encounter the famous Canon Episcopi, which is noted by Regino of Prüm sometime around 906 CE. Regino quotes from it in his efforts to inform agents of the Church about certain beliefs they are to oppose among the populace. In essence the Canon refers to "wicked women" who they believe ride on animals at night together with the goddess Diana. Their company includes living people and those who are dead. Regino is concerned that other people hearing such tales may believe in them and turn away from the Christian faith. He also fears they will "return" to the "errors" of the pagans.[23]

The Canon appears to indicate that some form of veneration of the goddess Diana was still active in the tenth century. It was apparently popular enough to concern the Church. Regino's fear that people may "return" to pagan ways seems to suggest the existence of a pre-Christian sect in which people of his time participated and then later converted to Christianity. He does not use the word "witch" in his writings, and yet the Canon Episcopi will later play a large part in the distortion of the witch figure.

In later versions of the Episcopi, we find the appearance of the name Herodias placed alongside Diana. Herodias is a biblical character connected to the slaying of John the Baptist, and in medieval tradition she becomes associated with witches. Historian Carlo Ginzburg points out that Burchard, Bishop of Worms, added "Herodias" to the name of Diana when referring to the earlier canon about Diana and her night followers.[24] Therefore, "Herodias" is not present in the original canon references to Diana and her followers. The addition changes the original theme and introduces an invented connection.

Ginzburg mentions that the Council of Trier in 1310 "set Herodiana alongside Diana," and here we see another intentional alteration of the original theme. He points out that in 1390 Friar Beltramino "inserted" a reference to Herodias that did not appear in the trial records concerning a woman named "Sibillia." All of this appears to be designed to connect Diana (and witches) with the infamy of a biblical character. It is an instrumental part of tying the witch figure to anti-Christian themes, an association that by the fifteenth century will lead to allegations of Devil worship. Let us note at this point that the Devil was not officially associated with witches and witchcraft.

The Devil is featured in witchcraft trials and commentaries from the mid-fifteenth century through the early eighteenth century. This is the official period in which witchcraft is not witchcraft without the Devil. However, this invented connection brewed and simmered centuries earlier. Historian Edward Peters notes that the literature for instructing novices in monasteries during the twelfth to thirteenth centuries placed significant emphasis on the nature of the Devil and his power to mislead people.[25] It was only a matter of time before the Devil and witchcraft would mate in the eyes of theologians.

The writings of theologian Alphonso Tostado (circa 1440) first introduce the notion (based upon the Canon Episcopi) that the pagan goddess Diana and the figure called Herodias are really demons. Another theologian by the name of Jordanes de Bergamo (circa 1470) wrote that demons have the ability to delude magicians and witches through their "three-fold power" to use illusion, dreams, and their capability to physically relocate people at will. These imaginings (if not deliberate inventions) became an increasing body of writings that fueled the fears of theologians in the following centuries.

Eventually the package was assembled giving demons a leader (Satan) and assigning a sect of followers (witches). It was a brilliant process resulting in the invention of an enemy of Christianity and setting the stage for a war of eradication. Fear of an enemy, real or imagined, has always functioned well for authorities. One of the tactic's advantages is that it works extremely well at directing people's attention away from the seriousness of social problems or covert operations. Europe during this period was plagued with everything from widespread disease to intense poverty to the financial collapse of its economic systems.

People will allow actions by the authorities that they would normally strongly oppose, as long as they feel such actions truly protect them from harm. They will even relinquish their rights granted in the society as long as they believe such rights will be returned once the enemy is vanquished. This tactic has worked for many centuries and is still in practice today. Fear eventually allowed the authorities to imprison, torture, and execute people falsely accused of the "crime" of witchcraft. Deaths numbered in the tens of thousands as people sat by and submitted to the rule of authority.

Among the footprints leading to the association of the Devil with witchcraft, we find the fashioned chain made from these links: sorcery with heresy, heresy with diabolism, diabolism with witchcraft, witchcraft with the Devil. The operative forge for this chain appears to originate around 1430. Over the next three decades it tempers the chain into a strong shackle that will bind witchcraft and the Devil together for centuries to come. Scholars Alan Kors and Edward Peters comment on this period and point to the regions of Europe in which the process begins, naming northwestern Italy, southeastern France, central and western Switzerland, and southwestern Germany.[26]

By the close of the Middle Ages the morphosis of the witch figure had already changed the perspectives of previous time periods. Many scholars refer to this as "the new idea of the witch" (as opposed to the invented idea). By the middle of the fifteenth century, "witchcraft" was fully heresy and was presented as such in public record. Ecclesiastical and lay authorities harshly prosecuted it as a crime. The Council of Basel transmitted the idea of this "new witchcraft" throughout Western Europe. The features of this invented form of witchcraft included charges of apostasy and a focused hatred toward Christian society. The strongest conviction though, was that all witches were collaborative servants of Satan. The dogs of war were unleashed upon the population.

Another feature of the fifteenth century is the notion that witches work in groups; in other words, they are a sect. Witches are then required to name other people belonging to their society. It is during this period that the idea of the witches' Sabbat becomes the standard of witchcraft and defines it in many minds. The basic idea of witches gathering together is not unique to the period; the unique elements are the formal gatherings called a Sabbat and the appearance of the Devil at such appointed times of revelry.

Two hundred years earlier, during the thirteenth century, a mural wall painting appeared in the Italian town known as Massa Marittima in the region of Siena. George Ferzoco (director of the center for Tuscan studies at the University of Leicester) refers to it as the earliest depiction in art of women acting as witches.[27] It was uncovered on August 6, 2000 after centuries of hiding. The large, richly colored painting—seven meters high—was found under layers of subsequent over-painting next to a fountain in the center of Massa Marittima. It shows a tall spreading tree with two groups of women standing beneath its branches. The first thing usually noticed about the tree is the unusual "fruit" hanging from its boughs. The fruit appears to be a crop of twenty-five phalluses.

Beneath the tree are two groups of women, one standing to the right and the other to the left side of the trunk of the tree. One of the women in the group on the left is holding up a stick with which she appears to be trying to dislodge a bird's nest. The mural features two of the other women grabbing each other's hair as they seem to fight for possession over one of the phalluses picked from the tree. It is noteworthy that no demons appear in the painting and the Devil is completely absent. This demonstrates that such concepts were not part of the depiction of the witches' gathering during this period.

The Inquisitors' manual known as the *Malleus Maleficarum* gives a description of witchcraft practices that includes witches robbing men of their genitals. The passage claims that witches sometimes collect male organs in great numbers (as many as twenty or thirty members). These are placed in a bird's nest or closed inside a box, where they come alive and are fed oats and corn. In Tuscan folklore there are tales about witches removing penises from men and placing them in bird's nests on tree branches, where they multiply and take on a life of their own. It is interesting to note that the Italian mural was painted two centuries earlier than the writing and publication of the *Malleus Maleficarum*.

One theory about the mural proposes it to be a unique piece of political propaganda commissioned by one Tuscan faction to sully the reputation of another. This idea points to a group known as the *Guelphs* who may have used the painting to warn that if the *Ghibellines* were allowed power they would bring with them heresy, sexual perversion, civic strife, and witchcraft. Surely if the Devil were part of the common beliefs about witchcraft in this period, his image would be featured in the painting for its impact on the message.

The Guelphs and Ghibellines were two factions that fought for power in Tuscany and northern Italy for decades during the Middle Ages. Perhaps the most famous victim of their feuds was the popular poet Dante. He was a Guelph expelled from his native Florence in 1302 after a rival Guelph group took power. At the time of the mural's painting, the Guelphs controlled Massa Marittima. It was their common practice, when launching attacks against the Ghibellines, to label them as heretics.

My personal view of the mural is more esoteric in nature than is the idea of it being a political billboard advertisement. If we accept that the mural is the earliest depiction in art of women acting as witches, then what does the imagery reveal about witchcraft beliefs in this period? There are several noteworthy aspects other than the absence of the Devil at this assembly of witches. The presence of a magical tree is an important element reflecting a long-standing tradition of the witches' tree at Benevento, Italy.

The depiction of witches assembled in the mural, along with the absence of the Devil, shares much in common with the early ideas of the witches' meetings. In the fifteenth-century sermons of Bernardino of Siena, we find what may be the first descriptions of witch assemblies in the Christian era. Bernardino uses the Italian term *tregenda* when referring to the assembly of witches. The gatherings had yet to be called Sabbats at this time in European history. Scholar Franco Mormando commented that Bernardino's sermons provide some ideas about the concept of regular witches' assemblies in this time period. He goes on to say that the roots of the Sabbat go back into pagan mythology related to the "un-Christian but non-diabolical" Society of Diana.[28]

Dominican preacher Jacopo Passavanti (circa 1354) wrote in his work titled *Lo Specchio della versa Penitenza* (The Mirror of True Repentance) that witch gatherings involved a belief in communicating with the dead. He refers to this meeting as a tregenda. His complaint is that witches take advantage of people who believe it is possible to speak with the dead. Passavanti states that witches are imposters who prey on the bereavement of other people for financial gain or out of sheer malice. He goes on to concede that some people may sincerely think they see dead people, but that in such cases they are actually seeing the Devil impersonating dead people.[29] This type of reasoning constantly forces the witch into a negative role. No allowances are ever granted that witches do anything other than for ill gain, deception, or evil intent. With such a filter in place, the investigation into actual practices of witchcraft can do nothing but fail to provide a balanced discernment. This is another reason why a true history of witches does not exist.

We have spent time examining some of the key influences in Southern and Western Europe that helped invent the official view of witchcraft. Now we will look north to the perception of witchcraft in the British Isles. It is not important to the purposes of this book whether the seeds of diabolical witchcraft blew in from the south or were indigenous to the northern region. In the final analysis the so-called history of witchcraft differs insignificantly whether we look at the British Isles or continental Europe. That being said, it should be noted that differences did exist. My point is that they were not of a nature that ultimately presented continental witchcraft and that of the British Isles as being significantly different practices overall.

In our comparison of regional witchcraft we must note that the etymological roots of the witch in English differ from its Southern European counterpart. The English word "witch" is derived from the Old English words *wicce* and *wicca*. These words relate to magic-users. Wicce is the female practitioner, and wicca is the male counterpart. In England the etymology attached to the witch does not appear to indicate an association with a supernatural concept (such as the strix). It also does not seem rooted in the knowledge of plants per se as is the Greek pharmakis. However, in later periods many of the continental beliefs about witches and witchcraft are found in English witchcraft.

Historian Alan MacFarlane points out various differences between English witchcraft and that of witchcraft in continental Europe. He notes, for example, that in the county of Essex witches are not accused of attending the Sabbat, dancing or feasting, or sexual perversion.[30] It appears that not until the activities of witch-hunter Matthew Hopkins (circa 1645) does English witchcraft bear a strong resemblance to the allegations made in French or German witchcraft trials.

The first statutes concerning witchcraft in English law were enacted in 1542. Prior to this time the "crimes" of magic were dealt with through various writs on a localized regional level. Complaints that the temporal laws were insufficient to deal with witchcraft resulted in the passage of the 1563 "Acts against Conjurations, Enchantments and Witchcraft." This set of laws introduced the death penalty and defined acts that were considered to be witchcraft. They included using magic to harm people or property and spells intended to provoke "unlawful love."

In 1604 a revised act included a law against consulting with "wicked" spirits as well as feeding them, using their aid, and rewarding them in any fashion. It also outlawed removing dead bodies from their graves. This gives us a good idea about beliefs related to the alleged behavior of witches in this time period. But were these acts actually performed by like-minded people in such great numbers as to warrant laws against them? This seems unlikely, and the simplest answer is to conclude that excessive exaggeration at best was at play here.

MacFarlane mentions a work titled *Guide to the Grand Jury Men*, written by Richard Bernard sometime around 1627. It provides a list of acceptable witnesses against people accused of witchcraft. Among the list we find inclusion of the "white witch" or "good witch." This indicates that the belief in a non-diabolical witch existed in England during this time period. Bernard does not describe the good witch, and the figure in this case may actually be nothing more than a type of Cunning Folk. However, MacFarlane does note what he suggests is an increasing interest in white witchcraft among authorities during the period from 1571 to 1586. He goes on to say that the white witch stood the risk of being accused of black witchcraft, and cites the case of Margery Skelton. She had been a witness in a witchcraft trial in 1566 to which she was summoned as a white witch to give testimony against the accused. In 1572 she was brought before the same court on charges of black witchcraft.

In an old work titled *A Discourse of the Damned Art of Witchcraft*, written by W. Perkins, we read the condemnation of the white witch. Author Christina Hole provides a quote from the text referring to the white witch as the "blessing witch." Perkins states this type of witch "deserves death" even more than the black witch. This is because while people avoid the black witch, they willingly go to the white witch for aid. Perkins states that in doing so, people reject the power of God and depend upon the white witch in matters of the divine.[31] Here again we see the means by which the character of the witch is always vilified no matter how positive it appears. It is ironic how the official truth tellers can manipulate things. This manipulation helps construct a distorted cultural reflection. In turn this supports the domination of popular beliefs that suppress the subculture possessing the previous or original model (obscuring it, if not completely burying it from sight without a trace).

In the early fifteenth century the lines of distinction between forms of practices such as sorcery, divination, and necromancy began to significantly blur. These separate ideas or practices eventually merge into one dark art practiced by those in alliance with the Devil. This became the antisocial sect redefined and labeled as witches. Its members were said to bear marks on their body to identify them as the Devil's own, and to sign a pact in their own blood. In exchange the members of the sect were said to receive a servant spirit who was a demon in disguise.

Once the new sect of witches was constructed and firmly established in the minds of theologians and various authorities, magical practices and practitioners were reinterpreted to conform to the diabolical vision. People in the past who would not have been viewed as witches at the time were now regarded as such. This revisionist history lent support to the depiction of witchcraft by the learned class. A greater, expanded vision of witchcraft took root, and in this vision, witches were now part of a vast conspiracy against human society and Christianity. The leader of these rebels was, of course, the Devil.

The Devil, like the witch, is a figure that has transformed over the centuries. Christian theologians assign him to the serpent in the Garden of Eden story. In this tale a talking snake appears on or near a specific tree (its kind is not named). In response to a question asked by the snake, Eve points out that God has forbidden eating the fruit of this tree, and if she eats the fruit, she will die. The snake replies to Eve that she will not die. It goes on to state that by eating the fruit her eyes will be open and she will know good and evil in the manner of God.

According to the tale, Eve then desires to eat the fruit in order to become wise. She eats it but does not die. Instead she comes to know good and evil, just as the serpent said would happen. Despite telling Eve the truth, the snake is vilified as a deceiver. This becomes the foundation of Satan as a liar. But in this tale the serpent does not lie. Curiously, it is Eve who disobeys God, and yet the serpent is the first to be punished for her disobedience.

As the story continues, God makes clothing for Adam and Eve and puts it on them to cover their naked bodies. Next God expresses a concern that the couple might eat from the "tree of life" and live forever. This appears to indicate that Adam and Eve did not originally possess that ability. Theologians point to the serpent's tempting of Eve, and the resulting eating of the fruit, as the means by which death enters into the human experience. But as we can see from the scripture, this does not conform to the chronology of the storyline.

As the tale continues, God drives Adam and Eve out of Eden and sets angels to guard against access to the tree of life. But we are still left with the problem that God told Eve she would die if she ate the fruit of the other tree. However, she remains alive, and the truth spoken by the snake (that she would not die) becomes the lie. I have always found that fascinating.

Later in the Book of Genesis we find a passage about the life span of humans. It appears in chapter five, which deals with the "sons of God" taking human wives. Offspring are born from this union, and God appears displeased. As a result he fixes the life span of humankind to one hundred twenty-five years. This is the first formal statement that God intentionally wants all humans to die, and he sets the clock for an inescapable appointment with death.

In popular tradition the story of the serpent in the Garden of Eden is different from the official text. People believe the serpent tricked Eve into eating the fruit, but looking at the story there is no trick or deception. The serpent simply states the facts. Popular belief holds that the serpent is responsible for the downfall of humankind in Eden. But in the story it is Eve who is responsible, although she does try to redirect the blame to the serpent. Here we see an example of how popular and learned tradition can differ. We also see how vilification can be a tool for unwarranted depictions of a figure that people need to view as evil for their own personal gain.[32] Coupling the witch with the Devil is an amplification of this principle. It was a diabolically clever tactic created and used by Christian theologians.

In this chapter we have investigated the evolution of the witch figure and how inventiveness contributed to the resulting stereotype. Notation has been made of the white witch, who may or may not have been one of the Cunning Folk. It is clear that ideas in the past shifted position and changed greatly concerning the nature and character of the witch figure. It is noteworthy that the image of the witch is still in transition. One of the major shifts is traceable to several authors in the early and mid-twentieth century. They were influenced by popular ideas arising in what scholars call the Romantic era of the nineteenth century.

Romancing the Witch

Let's visit the romantic notions about the witch that appear in the nineteenth and early twentieth century. These are not used as "proof text" to support the idea that such witches existed and operated at the time. They are included as positive views people held about witches in that era. Why should we accept only the negative depictions as "historical" and reject or ignore the positive as we discern the available data? After all, the latter is also part of the history of attitudes about witches and witchcraft. Therefore, it deserves at least a mention if not a revisit.

We have previously noted that one of the criticisms of Neo-Pagan writers is the allegation of inventing a positive view of witches and witchcraft in the past. This depiction is often called pseudo-history, which is closer to a polite way of saying fake.

However, the non-diabolical depiction of witches is not anything new or invented by Neo-Pagans. So we will look at some of these earlier positive views. I do not present them as proof of anything other than their existence in periods prior to the rise of Neo-Paganism.

If memory serves me correctly, sometime around 1970 or 1971, I first encountered a publication titled *The Witches' Almanac*. This was a delightful chance finding in a small market shop. Upon returning home and leafing through the booklet, I was struck to the core by a particular old passage. It read:

> "Hear ye then how our fathers before us discover'd the Witche:
>
> Mark well their manner, for it is quiet and assumeth naught. It is in peacefull tones they speak, and oft seem abstracted. Seeming to prefer the company of Beastes, they converse with them as equals.
>
> They will dwelle in lonely places, there better (as they say) to know the voices of the Wind and hear the secrets of Nature. Possessing Wysdom of the feldes and forrests, they doe heale and arme with their harvests.
>
> They concerne themselves not with idle fashion, nor doe worldly Goodes hold worth for them.
>
> Be not so confused as to think that only Womankynde harbour the gift in this matter. Of Men there bee many that holde mickle power" —Edward Johnston, Esq. Sudbery, Suffolk

My early days of training in witchcraft awoke something spiritual within me that I immediately identified in these words appearing in the almanac. There was a resonance, and I did not need the passage to be historical. The words simply felt right. However, it did begin a quest for me to find other writings of a similar nature. In retrospect, I think I needed the comfort of knowing I was not alone with the views of a handful of teachers who were around me while I was growing up. I was fascinated that people "out there" might also *know* this kindred spirit.

My quest was directed by a chance meeting in the summer of 1969 with a young woman who told me she practiced Wicca. As she revealed things to me about her practices, I discovered many similarities between Wicca and the witchcraft I had been previously taught. There were also differences, but they seemed insignificant at the time. Other doorways were opening, and I eagerly passed through them in my search for kindred witches.

In the early 1970s I was introduced to folkloric books written in the nineteenth century. They presented the idea of paganism in an intriguing light. There was also an undertone to them that was anti-Christian in nature. What appealed to me most was the message that the old ways were unjustly vilified in Christian culture. This felt like a personal vindication.

I still like to draw upon the works of nineteenth-century folklorists and other writers of the period. Criticism is sometimes directed at me for appreciating these works. The complaint is that the writers of this period (many of whom were Englishmen) did not understand the culture of other countries they visited and wrote about. Therefore, the interpretation of the customs and practices they witnessed is an inaccurate conclusion of their meaning and intent. True or not, what I value most is the raw data as compared to the interpretation of it by folklorists of the period. In other words, I look at the events as described in detail because they are historical eyewitness accounts. Although I do note the interpretation of the witnessed events, their conclusions mean less to me by comparison. Ultimately, what I want are the details, and I compare them with other customs and practices in various regions. The commonality speaks to me of old roots.

During my early years of research, I chanced upon references to Girolamo Tartarotti. His eighteenth-century work titled *Del Congresso Notturno delle Lammie*[33] was among the first written appearances of the word *stregheria*, which is an antiquated term in the Italian language and is translated into English as "witchcraft." Worthy of notice is Tartarotti's views on Diana and witchcraft. Two passages in particular stand out. The first appears on page 92 where he writes:

> Le moderne streghe adunque, che non sono da meno dell'antiche, nelle ragioni delle quelle succedettero, debbono per conseguenza godere tutti I diritti e privilege, che quelle godevano.

> (The assembly of modern witches is nothing less than the ancient ones, and because of this succession they enjoy all the rights and privileges of their ancestors.)

And on page 165 we find:

> Che le nostrè Streghe sono una derivazione, e propagine dell' antiche seguaci di Diana, e di Erodiade, e che il delitto dell' une e dell' altre in sostanza è lo stesso.[34]

> (The witches of our time are derived from, and are the offspring of, the ancient ones, who were followers of Diana, and Erodiade, and that their crime is witchcraft, just as it was in the past.)

Tartarotti was admonished by the Church for depicting witches in a way conflicting with the Church's teachings, in which the latter presented witches as worshippers of the Devil (and not a goddess). This resulted in a retraction that came in the form of a revision published in 1751 under the title *Apologia del Congresso Notturno delle Lammie*. Modern scholars reject Tartarotti's views of witches as a Dianic sect because he offers no evidence to support the claim, and because no one else in his time period supported the idea. This attitude declares that a lack of proof equals non-existence, and an unshared conclusion contains no truth. Such a perspective is very convenient for those eager to dismiss other possibilities that do not coincide with their own conclusions.

Despite Tartarotti's rejection by modern scholars, his view was certainly rooted in the pre-Christian literary tradition of witches and Diana. Naturally, this does not prove that such a relationship existed, but it should soften criticism aimed at Tartarotti as though he created the notion himself. Even in the Christian era, the goddess Diana shows up in commentaries that demonstrate her continued veneration among country people. The Canon Episcopi is not the only example, and the veneration of Diana is noted by St. Martin in his sixth-century travels through the northwestern regions of the Iberian peninsula. Martin's references to Diana in the sixth century, the canon's concern about Diana in the tenth century, and Tartarotti's opinion in the eighteenth century verify a long-standing theme that appears reluctant to disappear or to transform itself into Devil worship. The latter becomes the work of the Church.

Folklorist Jacob Grimm once commented, in his work *Deutsche Mythologie*, that "The witches belong to the retinue of ancient goddesses, who—fallen from their thrones and changed from good and adorable beings to fiendish and fearful ones—wander restlessly about during the hours of night, and in place of the old festive processions hold secret unlawful meetings with their adherents."[35] It is interesting to see a shift in the depiction of the witch especially by a writer who published fairy tales in which witches seek to harm children.

The nineteenth-century French historian Jules Michelet once wrote "Witches they are by nature. It is a gift peculiar to woman and her temperament. By birth a fay, by the regular recurrence of her ecstasy she becomes a sibyl. By her love she grows into an enchantress. By her subtlety, by a roguishness often whimsical and beneficent, she becomes a Witch; she works her spells; does at any rate lull our pains to rest and beguile them."[36] Michelet is rejected by scholars due to a belief that he possessed a strong political prejudice and a lively imagination.

As we continue to look at romantic notions of the witch, we cannot bypass the commentary of Edward Carpenter who, in his book *Intermediate Types among Primitive Folk*, writes:

Karl Pearson, assuming the real prevalence of these institutions in early times points out, reasonably enough, that when Christianity became fairly established matriarchal rites and festivals, lingering on in out-of-the-way places and among the peasantry, would at once be interpreted as being devilish and sorcerous in character, and the women (formerly priestesses) who conducted them and perhaps recited snatches of ancient half-forgotten rituals, would be accounted witches. "We have, therefore," he says, "to look upon the witch as essentially the degraded form of the old priestess, cunning in the knowledge of herbs and medicine, jealous of the rites of the goddess she serves, and preserving in spells and incantations such wisdom as early civilization possessed." This civilization, he explains, included the "observing of times and seasons," the knowledge of weather-lore, the invention of the broom, the distaff, the cauldron, the pitchfork, the domestication of the goat, the pig, the cock and the hen, and so forth—all which things became symbols of the witch in later times, simply because originally they were the inventions of woman and the insignia of her office, and so the religious symbols of the Mother-goddess and her cult.[37]

Carpenter's view is very similar to that of Neo-Pagans in their depiction of a matrifocal (if not matriarchal) goddess cult in which they feel a sense of spiritual connective roots.

The Neo-Pagan position of the witch as a priestess is nothing new.[38] Ancient writers portrayed Medea as a priestess of Hecate. A grandiose depiction of the priestess witch appears in the 1893 publication of a book titled *Woman, Church and State: A Historical Account of the Status of Woman through the Christian Ages.* Its author, Matilda Joslyn Gage, wrote:

> Henry Moore, a learned Cambridge graduate of the seventeenth century wrote a treatise on witchcraft explanatory of the term "witch" which he affirmed signified a wise, or learned woman. The German word 'hexe' that is, witch, primarily signified priestess, a wise or superior woman who in a sylvan temple worshipped those gods and goddesses that together governed earth and heaven. Not alone but with thousands of people for whom she officiated she was found there especially upon Walpurgis night, the chief Hexen (witch) Sabbat of the north.[39]

This image reminds me of modern Pagan festivals where it is not uncommon for witches to facilitate rituals for the gathered attendees.

For one last look at early twentieth-century views, we turn to *The Book of Witches*, by Oliver Madox Hueffer. The author writes:

> With the first introduction of civil government the witch and the priestess finally part company, to range themselves henceforward upon opposite sides. It is true that as religion follows religion the

priestess of the former era often becomes the witch of its successor, thereby only accentuating the distinction. For, in the unceasing efforts to arrange a modus vivendi between the human and the supernatural worlds, the priestess accommodates herself to circumstances—the witch defies them. The priestess, acknowledging her own humanity, claims only to interpret the wishes of the god, to intercede with him on behalf of her fellow-men. The witch, staunch Tory of the old breed, claims to be divine, in so far as she exercises divine power unamenable to human governance, and thus singles herself out as one apart, independent of civil and ecclesiastical powers alike—and as such an object of fear and of suspicion. Even so she is still respectable, suspect indeed, but not condemned. The public attitude towards her is variable; she is alternately encouraged and suppressed, venerated and persecuted—and through all she flourishes, now seductive as Circe, now hag-like as was Hecate.[40]

In this writing we see a returning tinge of the old sting—the witch as antisocial and defiant. She is a rebel against any creed, doctrine, or dogma that attempts to control her.

To my knowledge the first full-scale attempt to romanticize the witch is rooted in the writings of anthropologist Margaret Murray. She is well known for her theory that European witchcraft was the cult of Diana that survived into the Christian era. A series of her books on the subject expanded the idea of a simple peasant religion into a much more encompassing organization. The latter included members of royalty, and this was the final straw for her academic colleagues (who were very skeptical to begin with when her first book on witchcraft was published).

Today Murray's views are completely rejected by contemporary scholars. Individual pieces of historical witchcraft and bits of authentic witch lore uncovered in her research are now automatically rejected because her overall thesis is disputed. No one gets absolutely everything wrong, yet anyone who so much as hints that a single line from Murray's work may have value instantly loses credibility. To quote her in any supportive way, no matter how small, is now the equivalent of finding a fly floating in the soup. Everything gets dumped.

The writings of Murray were still influential in the early days of the formation of Wicca, which during the first half of the nineteenth century was known as witchcraft. A man named Gerald Gardner publicized witchcraft as a surviving pagan religion in England, and Murray wrote the introduction in his book *Witchcraft Today*. The roots of modern Wicca are traceable to Gardner and others of his era. Author and witch Raymond Buckland is credited with later introducing Wicca into the United States.

Prior to the 1980s the words *witchcraft* and *Wicca* were synonymous. Both were often referred to as the *Old Religion*, the *Craft of the Wise*, or simply as the *Craft*. Witchcraft and Wicca are traditionally initiatory systems, meaning that in order to become a member you have to be brought in and taught by someone already trained and knowledgeable in the arts. Very little was known publicly about witchcraft or Wicca for several decades following its surfacing in the 1950s. The few books available on the topic were written by people on the inside or by those who interviewed initiated witches. Or so it was all presented at the time.

With the writings of such authors as Scott Cunningham, the idea of Wicca began to change, at least in the United States. Formal training and initiation became deemed as unnecessary. In the following decade many people even regarded them as undesirable. This environment was fertile for the establishment of self-styled systems, self-initiation, and the formation of eclectic "traditions" of Wicca. A new paradigm displaced the model of witchcraft or

Wicca of the previous decades, and individuals relied upon the approach of "whatever feels right" as opposed to traditional training concepts and methods. The idea of a "witchcraft tradition" itself fell from favor and became viewed as a shackle instead of a firm foundation.

The decade of the 1990s brought even more change to witchcraft. The terms *Wicca* and *witchcraft* formally split into two different definitions. Wicca became the religion of witches, and witchcraft was now separately its magical practice. This idea also weakened, and the notion rose that Wiccans and witches are not automatically the same thing.

In England less modification took place in terms of Wicca and witchcraft. One example is what is often referred to as British Traditional Wicca (BTW). It is comprised of traditions tracing their lineage from hereditary or old British sources. These include the Gardnerian and Alexandrian traditions as well as several branches and offshoots. Among them we find the New Forest coven associated with Sybil Leek, the Clan of Tubal Cain (of Robert Cochrane fame) and Plant Bran. Some BTW groups feel that the term *Wicca* belongs strictly to the Craft in England and should not be used by people without traceable lineage. Others apply the word to only Gardnerian and Alexandrian groups and their offshoots. In the United States the word applies to any system related to the ideas and concepts that came from the British Isles regardless of modification.

The decades of the 1960s and 1970s (often associated with the Hippie movement) brought about a reversal in conservative modes of thinking; it was an era of challenging authority and conventional views. The idea of the witch as a Devil worshipper gave way to a new generation, which saw the witch as misunderstood and maligned. These decades presented the witch as involved in an ancient fertility cult connected to a mother goddess and an antlered god of nature. At the core of this concept was the belief that witchcraft survived underground as a secret society. It was not uncommon for people to claim a long-standing family tradition of witchcraft. Such claims later declined as we passed into the 1990s and on into current times.

In the following chapter we will turn our attention to discovering the witch figure free from invented ideas. Our goal is to set aside the preconceived notions and look at less contaminated ideas. Although we still have to wade through past beliefs and attitudes, the cracks and holes in the wall provide a view of what has long been hidden away. We can now clear away the debris and recover the missing pieces.

Chapter Three

UNEARTHING THE WITCH

We have examined the witch as depicted through the schemes of those who benefited from the image of the diabolical witch. While this invention is certainly the best-known portrayal, there are other less prejudicial perspectives to consider. Many of them can be found in a variety of sources that are secondary to the writings specifically targeting witchcraft.

Now we will look at themes appearing in various accounts, tales, and legends related to witches and witchcraft. One of the goals is to separate the impossible from the possible, which will give us a clearer image of the witch in the past (and the present). In doing so, we will focus on the witch as a real person capable of performing feasible activities. This will help us separate out the contrived witch and arrive at something more useful to our discernment.

Throughout this chapter we will highlight the reappearing components that surface in witchcraft trial accusations (excluding such things as the fantastic elements of flight and physical transformation). The idea is to look at folkloric elements and bits of witch lore that can exist on their own without a connection to witchcraft as evil or as defined by a pact with the Devil. We will also take a brief look at things that are too often ignored or dismissed in order to perpetrate the notion of witchcraft as a form of Devil worship or a Christian heresy.

There is one very important thing missing in our understanding of the witch figure of the past. This is the word used by witches themselves for identification. If we knew this name, then it could provide us with vital insights, particularly in terms of etymology. Unfortunately, we know only the names used by non-witches to refer to people believed to be witches. One possible exception appears in the field studies of nineteenth-century folklorists investigating witchcraft in Italy.[41] To my knowledge these are the first reports taken directly from people identifying themselves as witches and who were willing to talk about their practices without coercion. In Italian the word commonly translated into "witch" is *strega* (female witch) and *stregone* (male witch).

Many scholars dismiss these field studies because the data do not comply with the stereotypes that define witchcraft in the academic community. Another reason for dismissal is that the accepted academic methodology of contemporary scholars was not refined in the nineteenth century. Therefore, most modern scholars consider the data collected directly from interviewed witches of this period to be unreliable. Scholars prefer instead to stand by the official "history" of witchcraft, which depicts a sect of witches who we can be reasonably certain never existed at all.

In chapter one, we looked at the etymology of the earliest word for witch in Western culture. As we discovered, the word is *pharmakis* (a word related to the knowledge of plant substances). Other words were to follow, and one such word became the foundation of the invented witch figure we have today. This word is *strix*, a Latin word indicating a screech owl. This suggests that people living in the era of this word's usage believed in a connection between the witch and the screech owl. The connection may stem from ritual cries once made by witches in the night, or the association may be more mythical in nature.[42] Could it be that some witches referred to themselves as the *owl people*? The precedent of taking on tribal animal names does exist in pre-Roman Italy. Some examples include tribes that took the names *Piceni* (woodpecker), *Lucani* (wolf), and *Ursenti* (bear). This practice is tied to the myth of the animal guide, or ancestor, feeder, and protector (a widespread belief in prehistoric Italy).[43]

In chapter two we noted ancient writings depicting a supernatural creature called a *striga* that was a type of vampire owl. According to old lore this creature was able to transform itself into the figure of an old woman. In the lore of the period, the striga preyed on newborn babies, small children, and women. Over the course of time, both strix and striga became terms for a witch. Some scholars make a distinction between the supernatural, or "night-witch," and the human witch that people may actually have encountered in real day-to-day life. Historian Richard Gordon notes such a distinction in ancient times.[44] He goes on to say that the depiction of the witch as one who poisons is a created blending of the wise-woman and root-cutter figures, and not an ethnological account.

According to most scholars the words *striga* or *strix* evolved into the word *strega*. Its contemporary usage in mainstream Italian culture is always negative, just as it was in the past. If striga and strix are the roots of the modern word *strega*, then it is reasonable to assume that the notion of the creature indicated by these terms has long contaminated ideas about the actual witch figure over the centuries. Some people believe that the presence of a supernatural creature in ancient cultural beliefs about witches negates the idea that a human witch also existed in the minds of the populace. But this erroneous assessment is contrary to the academic view as noted in the comments by Gordon.

From time to time the argument surfaces that people would not use a name for themselves that is regarded as negative in the culture in which they are raised. People with this view reject the idea that anyone in the past self-identified as a witch (or in the case of Italians, as a strega or stregone). However, we do know that some people today embrace the name "witch" in the United States and Britain despite its negative meaning in mainstream culture. We also know that minorities will call each other by names that other people use as derogatory remarks (I refer to racist slurs). So the argument is weak when we look at the example of people in our own time. Modern witches face many of the same social perils today as did those in past ages. Granted, it is no longer legal to imprison, torture, and execute people accused of witchcraft (at least in most countries), but significant consequences still remain. Despite this, we do find people openly identifying themselves as witches. We also find people privately referring to themselves as witches. This strongly suggests that mainstream definitions and attitudes are not necessarily a deterrent.

Throughout the course of this chapter, we will look at various themes related to witches depicted as real people. We will also examine references to witchcraft that are meant to indicate a feasible practice as opposed to impossible supernatural events. My intent is not to claim them as proof of anything per se. I use them instead to present beliefs held by various people in different eras.

The question becomes why these beliefs persist through the ages despite contrary ones that form the official accepted views about witches and witchcraft.

Among the most persistent references are mentions of a goddess in witchcraft trials and in commentaries by various Church officials and other so-called authorities on the subject. The names of these goddesses are naturally those of the region in which they appear, at least for the most part. However, the Roman goddess Diana is frequently found outside of Italy and particularly in the German records. Other types of goddesses are mentioned in Eastern Europe. For example, scholar Éva Pócs reports thirty-six documented cases in Hungarian witchcraft trial transcripts that involve a "fate goddess."[45] The fact that these trials span three centuries is a remarkable testimony to the persistence of goddess themes in witchcraft accusations.

Scholar Carlo Ginzburg, in his book *Ecstasies: Deciphering the Witches' Sabbat*, provides us with a chapter titled "Following the Goddess." Here we find the names of several female divinities that appear in trial transcripts as early as 1390 and then onward into the following centuries. The names include Diana, Bensozia, Herodias, Madonna Horiente/Oriente, Bona Domina, Richella, Habonde, Abundia, Unholde, Bethe, Helt, Doamna Zinelor, Irodiada, Arada, Satia, and the unnamed "Queen of Elves" (however, Ginzburg states that the names are not reliable as some may have been assumed and others deliberately inserted into the records).

As noted in chapter one, the goddess Diana appears in connection with witchcraft in the works of the Roman poet known as Horace. The witches in his writings are associated with Diana, who witnesses their rites. They use magic and possess books containing enchantments that can draw down the moon and stars.

Horace depicts the witch as completely human, and we do not find accounts of flying or changing physical form. We do, however, clearly see descriptions of heinous acts. Grave-robbing is one of the accusations made against witches in Horace's era.

Many modern people would likely be shocked at the idea of gathering bones from graveyards. Horace and other ancient writers frequently refer to this taking place. In ancient times the graveyards of the poor consisted of shallow graves, and it was not uncommon for animals to dig up the remains. I have no doubt that magic-users (witches included) took advantage of bones found exposed and scattered about the graveyard. Bones have long been used in magic for a variety of purposes, including using them in powdered form for potions and ointments as well as utilizing the marrow to make candles.

I am positive if we somehow traveled back in time we would not find ancient witches who believed in the "harm none" philosophy of popular contemporary Wicca. I also have no doubt that many modern witches would be unsettled by the ancient practice of witchcraft. At some point in history people practiced human sacrifice and animal sacrifice. Witches, as part of that ancient culture, almost certainly did so as well. Human society evolved and human sacrifice passed away as an acceptable act, but the anti-witch writings want us to believe that witches continued to practice live sacrifice through the ages. How likely is it that European culture evolved in this fashion but left the witch behind in such a significant way?

While the vilification of the witch does present us with difficulties in ferreting out a realistic view of her or him, there are traces of authentic practices referenced in trial documents, to which we can turn for some answers. Among the practices attributed to witches is the making of love potions and healing through primitive forms of magic.[46] It is here that we catch a glimpse of the witch in a non-diabolical presentation. Naturally, the anti-witch sees such services as devious and self-serving, but as we noted in chapter two, the witch is never given the benefit of the doubt. Everything she or he does is always interpreted in the worst possible light.

Scholar Owen Davies presents us with a depiction of what he calls the beggar witch. In his book *Witchcraft, Magic, and Culture 1736–1951*, we find several examples of people he calls beggar witches; one example is a woman named Old Dolly who is reportedly a witch from Shropshire (pointy hat and all).[47] According to Davies some of the beggar witches intentionally performed harmful acts in retribution for being denied donations. This increased their reputation for magic, which in turn inspired people not to ignore the beggar. Here we are looking at the peasant witch trying to survive, which is a more realistic view than that of an inherently evil witch who is always looking to harm someone for the sheer enjoyment of it.

Davies points out that the beggar witch did not identify herself as a witch within her community. It is inferred that people knew who the witch was (real or imagined). But for the witch to directly threaten anyone would reduce her to an extortionist, which would not be tolerated. Therefore, it was not actually the fear of the witch that caused people to offer her sustenance. It was a desire to remain in her goodwill. Her goodwill meant aid in times of magical need. The witch has always been the last resort when customary methods failed.

Certain themes reappear over the centuries as recorded in trial transcripts throughout Europe. Among the most common we find accusations of potion making, spell casting, and the creation of wax or clay images of people for magical purposes. These are all very ancient practices, and their appearance in witchcraft demonstrates that the witch is a practitioner of magic in very common ways. It is here that we can see the witch as a real person involved in real practices.

The use of objects or items in witchcraft is a common theme. Some involved the use of a fig being touched to a skin problem. The fig is left out to decay and dry up in the belief that so too will the ailments. Some witches were accused of stealing the communion wafer from a church and adding it to their potions. This shows the witch as adaptive, a person who uses objects because they are associated with power. In such acts the witch believes that she or he can employ and direct powerful objects, even those others might feel should deter the witch from handling them. It is in examples such as this that we see the human witch as opposed to the folkloric or diabolical witch.

Historical records indicate that 91 percent of accused witches were women. Scholars have put various theories forth regarding this, but they all fail to take into account the most obvious reason. Women have always been the tradition keepers and the social community preservers. Traditionally, men concern themselves less in such matters. Of course when we generalize, we overlook the individuals that do not fit the stereotype, but it is in the idea of keeping traditions that things like witchcraft are sure to be passed on.

Examining the charges of witchcraft aimed largely at women, it is notable that the majority of them were elderly. Widows appear to be a popular victim. In fact, anyone generally disliked in a town or village was at great risk of being accused of practicing witchcraft. When we look at local folklore sources, we find many accounts of people being thought to be witches or remembered as having been a witch. Some scholars use the information contained in folktales to conclude that people reported to be witches were indeed witches.

Cultural historian Owen Davies states that folktales can be divided into two main categories: folk narratives and folk legends. According to Davies, folk narratives reflect popular beliefs presented through invented stories, whereas folk legends impart events that are believed to be true.[48] He goes on to say that the individuals who are said to be witches are real people, and in many cases can be traced to parish records. Davies appears to believe that if someone claimed to personally know a witch, or was told by a parent or grandparent that the person was a witch, then the person in question is one. I am not so easily persuaded to agree.

Davies does go on to say that care must be taken to ensure the reliability of the informant providing the folk legend. He states that an unreliable informant is one who has something to personally gain by passing on the story (a reward of some kind). By contrast, Davies's reliable witness is someone who (without obvious gain) passes on tales that conform to the stereotype of the evil witch. For Davies, a person's belief in the truth of the tale being told, and its depiction of the witch-character in keeping with negative core beliefs about witchcraft, makes the account trustworthy. I personally see nothing more here than the transmission and continuation of stereotypes applied to people who are in disfavor with their community. They may or may not have practiced some form of magic, and the person on the receiving end of the magic may well have regarded the results as undesirable, but the practice of magic for whatever purpose does not, by itself, make someone a witch.

From the late Middle Ages on, the Devil (or more specifically a pact with him) is the key indicator of a witch. The idea comes much later to England than does its continental introduction, but over time the witch and the Devil are inseparable in the British Isles as well. However, another component of witchcraft emerges related to bloodlines.

Davies comments that the belief in the hereditary witch is noted in Cornwall, circa 1855.[49] But such a belief is found in earlier periods as well. In the *Compendium Maleficarum*, we find a passage stating that it is "certain proof of guilt" if the accused has parents found guilty of practicing witchcraft. This is referred to as inheriting the "taint" of witchcraft. Davies notes the past belief that the "power of witchcraft" is passed through generations by the inheritance of witches' books. In such beliefs we begin to move away from the invented witch and draw closer to the type of witch who actually existed.

One historical figure worthy of examination is a woman called Biddy Early. She lived in Ireland, where she was born in 1798. Her given name was Bridget Ellen Connors, but she later took her mother's maiden name. Biddy grew up in poverty and lived on a small farm. Her mother had a reputation as an herbalist who made remedies for various ailments. From her mother, Biddy learned the art of making potions.

According to her legend, when Biddy was ten years old she one day encountered Faeries while collecting herbs, berries, and moss. This took place near two standing stones in a field where old legends told of Faery gatherings. In Biddy's day a "white thorn bush" grew near the stones. People were later to say that Biddy appeared to be talking to someone unseen whenever she visited this place. When asked about it, she replied that she spoke with Faeries that were teaching her things.[50] Because she was a child, this behavior did not concern her neighbors enough to take any actions.

Biddy spent much time with the Faery people in what she called her Faery corners. In later life she was known as a healer and as a person who could foretell events. People came to call her a wise woman. But it was during the time she resided in Dromore, near Kilbarron, that she came to be known as a witch.

At this point in her story a popular element arises. Biddy is known to possess a special bottle that had been prophesied by the spirit of her dead mother in a visitation years before. The bottle reportedly came from the Faery people. It was described as being about nine inches in height with a six-inch stem. The lower body of the bottle was bulbous, and the glass is described as blue in color (although some accounts report it being black). When not in use, Biddy always kept the bottle wrapped in a red cloth. Whenever she traveled, Biddy hid the bottle under a shawl.

The stories tell us that Biddy used the bottle like a scrying mirror. She would gaze at it and foretell the future for whoever sought out her services. She also provided small bottles containing potions for healing and other things that came up in her visions. Although people offered her money, she turned them down and instead accepted "gifts in kind" as payment.

As her popularity increased, Biddy came into conflict with the local Catholic clergy. The priests accused her of being in league with the Devil and spoke against her by name during the Sunday services in the local church. At one particular sermon the priest demanded that no one in the parish inform a stranger as to where Biddy lived (because people came from all around to seek her cures).

The problem for the priests was that Biddy's magic worked. She could do things that the priests could not, such as healing people, animals, and crops. When people were in need, they went to Biddy and not to the clergy of the Church. This only added to the animosity the priests felt toward her. It is even reported that the priests would not give absolution of sins to anyone in the parish who so much as talked with Biddy.

On several occasions a priest went to Biddy's house to confront her as an agent of the Devil, despite the fact that she was not known for harming anyone or anything. One priest entered her home and walked about snapping the lash of his whip to frighten Biddy. Upon leaving her home, the priest told Biddy that if he returned she would remember him now. Biddy replied that the priest would remember her too in just a short time. According to the story, when the priest rode away on his horse an incident took place on a narrow bridge. The horse stopped and refused to move. The priest then discovered that his feet were trapped in the stirrups. Neither he nor the horse was going anywhere. The priest ended up sending a passerby to Biddy's house with an apology and a promise never to bother her again. Biddy released the spell, and the priest hurried away.

In 1865 Biddy was charged with witchcraft under a 1586 statute. In court no one would testify against her, and the authorities were forced to release her for lack of evidence. The life story of Biddy Early ends in a peculiar way. On her deathbed in 1874 a lifelong friend (Pat Loughnane) convinced her to make peace with the Church. A priest named Father Connellan came to administer the last rites of the Catholic Church. During the process a crow kept flying into the window. At one point, the window was opened and the crow flew in and sat on the footboard of

Biddy's bed until she took her last breath. It then cawed and flew out the window.

Biddy reportedly passed her magical bottle on to the priest saying that the power now belonged to him. This is classic witch lore, which states that a witch cannot die until her or his witch powers are passed on to someone else. This can be performed through trickery in cases where the person does not want to receive the witch's power. In the case of Biddy's priest, it is said that he cast the bottle into Kilbarron Lake, where it was never found again.

The accounts of Biddy's life are important in showing some of the classic elements of Old World witchcraft. Her associations with the Faery people as teachers, along with the possession of a central and special object connecting her with magical power, are markers also found in Old Ways witchcraft. So too is Biddy's strong opposition to the Christian clergy when they misrepresent witches and practice anti-witchcraft behavior.

There are many examples of people believed to be witches who are eagerly sought out. Stories about them are not associated with evil acts or ill intentions. Author Lina Gordon, in her book *Home Life in Italy: Letters from the Apennines*, mentions an encounter with a mortal witch. She writes:

> The witch of flesh and blood, to whom the disappointed lovers go, to weave strange spells and brew love potions, live in quiet back streets in the towns or are to be found in isolated hill villages. One old fortune-teller, a real strega, I found at Carrara. La Violante lived in a low quarter of the town, to which Mariannina's cousin refused to conduct us, but one morning we escaped his vigilance and paid her a hasty visit. Her one room gave on a side road, and through the half-open door we saw a bed, a bare table,

and a little charcoal range; the lintel was guarded by a small bas-relief of the Madonna. Dressed in a patched gown, a tawny kerchief on her head, beneath which fell a few wisps of white hair, La Violante looked as poor as her lair. But Mariannina says that a good many soldi are hidden away somewhere, for she has an appointment for every moment of the day and no one gives her "less than twopence and sometimes they give her a silver franc."

She shot stealthy glances at me and kept up a running commentary as she threw the greasy cards in fantastic patterns upon the table: "Oh, I tell the truth—proprio la verita—and if you come on Friday the cards go best of all. My clients all know that La Violante is as good as her word, they are not always so good at keeping a bargain. Only the other day I foretold that a Signora would give birth to a son. 'Now, Violante,' she said, 'if you are right I'll give you a new cloak.' Well, the Signora got her son but I never got my cloak" And her eyes twinkled, though she shook her head sadly.

"Fiori, fiori, fiori" mumbled Violante as she turned up the court cards, "and they are all fiori del Morettino," for the dark-haired knave always appeared at every cut of the pack.

"Do you know a Morettino who is in love with you?" and she turned on me a searching look, but she evidently did not expect me to answer so compromising a question.

"My husband is fair," I remarked.

"Yes, there is a Biondino too, but Ecco il Morettino, who loves you well: here are letters to delight you and all good things, always from the Morettino, Flowers, flowers, flowers, from the little dark one."

The absurd thing was that Violante predicted I should receive a letter containing a sum of money, which was to be entirely for myself, and within a fortnight I received a small and totally unexpected legacy, which arrived by cheque in a letter. Consequently,

Mariannina now believes more than ever in La Violante, and keeps a sharp look out for the Morettino.[51]

During the nineteenth century, folklorist J.B. Andrews interviewed people claiming to be witches. From his field studies we find several interesting things appearing in his article titled "Neapolitan Witchcraft." Andrews writes:

> Southern Italy has been for many ages the favorite country for witches; they come from all parts of the peninsula to the Grand Councils held under the walnut-tree of Benevento, and even from more distant lands, for its fame is celebrated in Mentonnese tradition . . .

> The meetings take place at midnight in the country, when the witches dance and take council together . . .[52]

Andrews notes that, according to the witches he interviewed, witchcraft consists of separate Arts: "There are special departments of the art—there is that of the earth and of the sea—having their special adepts."

Later in the article Andrews mentions spells that are performed using the stars. On page five he reports that witches use three cords to invoke aid from the stars; one black, one red, and one white. The cords are knotted for various purposes, and pins are inserted into the knots to fix the spell in place. Andrews also notes the use of the witch's shadow in magical workings. This practice during the Renaissance is also noted by historian Ruth Martin in her book *Witchcraft and the Inquisition in Venice 1550–1650*. The theme is mentioned earlier by folklorist Charles Leland in his "Legend of Intialo," which all suggests a long-standing magical tradition.

The preservation of magical traditions by witches is a theme we find throughout the field studies of various folklorists in Italy during the nineteenth century. Andrews notes:

> The foregoing information was obtained quite recently from witches in Naples. When asked what books they used, they answered none, that their knowledge is entirely traditional.

Family traditions also feature prominently in these field studies. Andrews writes:

> An instruction in the methods is by itself sufficient; it is frequently given by the mother to her daughter. . . when a new witch has completed her education, the two women open a vein in their arms; having mixed the blood, the older witch makes a cross with it under the left thigh of her pupil.

So far in this chapter we have looked at examples of witches as actual people. We have seen their ways as realistic in comparison with the stereotypes of the diabolical witch in league with the Devil. But in order to understand the witch figure we must look to the mystical side of the witch as well, for the witch has two natures and can be separated into what I call the witch in sunlight and the witch in moonlight. The former refers to the witch as a person in her or his daily life. The latter reveals the witch as a mystic, and in this we see her or his connection to a realm that truly separates the witch from the average person.

The Enchanted World of the Witch

To better understand the witch figure, we need to look to more than just the daily affairs of the witch. Our attention should also go to her or his enchanted worldview, which we will explore here. For simplicity in this section I will use "she" and "her" when referring to a witch, and ask that it be understood not to exclude men. It is in revealing the mystical world of the witch that we begin to learn about her perceived relationship to it all. The witch's interaction with such realms guides her actions. Knowing why the witch performs a specific act is more enlightening than simply looking at the results. The witch is not without ethics, as many would claim. But in reality it is simply difficult for someone who is harmed to take responsibility for provoking the witch to begin with.

Even more realistic ideas of witches and their practices are found in the period following the decline in the belief of the witches' Sabbat and diabolical revelry. As reason began to direct the minds of both the learned and the uneducated, people were better able to see the very human witch who lived in or near their villages and towns. We see signs of this in the eighteenth century, and by the late nineteenth century, the witch appears as a fairly believable character. Remnants of old superstitions did still pop up, but they no longer resulted in hysteria and the killing of the witch. However, fear, misunderstanding, and ignorance remained firmly in place.

The type of witch who is the subject of this book is fully human and yet is often associated with the so-called supernatural world. This is where tales of the witch and the Faery merge together, and such tales are often inextricably interwoven. The concept appears throughout Europe with little significant difference. Sicilian folklorist Giuseppe Pitrè once noted that it is difficult to clearly distinguish between a Faery and a witch in the old tales. Old woodcuts depict Faery mounds that are also featured in tales about witches and Faery contact. These mounds are often located on or near prehistoric sites that are still associated with folk legends.

It is noteworthy that some of the witchcraft trials mention specific places where prehistoric gathering sites are located. At these sites we find barrows, dolmens, and megalithic monuments. Some people accused of witchcraft spoke of visits to these places where they met with Faeries. One particularly interesting account comes from a man named John Walsh who was tried for witchcraft in 1566. Walsh informed his examiners that he learned witchcraft from the Faeries whom he met at a barrow. His story included details about three types of Faeries: white, green, and black. The latter he regarded as very troublesome.

In 1623 a woman named Isabel Haldane, who was accused of being a witch, reported that she discovered the "faery land" in a hollow hill. Another accused individual, Jacob Behmen, was tried in 1654 and also spoke of gaining access to the realm of the Faeries by knocking three times on a Faery hill. One other example is that of Isobel Gowdie, accused of witchcraft in 1664. She admitted to visiting a Faery place known as Downie Hill where she claimed to feast with the king and queen of the Faeries.

French folklorist Émile Nourry (pseudonym Pierre Saintyves) investigated areas in the vicinity of megalithic monuments to see if stories existed linking them to accounts of witchcraft. He was intrigued that many bore names suggesting these places were once gathering sites for the practice of witchcraft. One particular site at Vaumont is named *La Pierre du Sabbat*, which suggests an association with witches' gatherings. Another is named *La Cusine des Sorciers* (The Sorcerer's Kitchen) and is attached to legends that witches used this site to make their potions.

Modern witches are drawn to using ancient sites associated with ritual and magical practices. One reason is that something mystical seems to call from there to the inner spirit. It is intuitively felt as a place of power or a connection to a meeting place between this world and the next. If witches met in days of old at these ancient sites, the reasons may have been similar. Perhaps it was simply a way of trying to return home to the world as it was before the One God came to displace the Many.

Some of the old sites have been connected to reported UFO activity. An associate of my mine who is an anthropologist once pointed out the similarities between UFO lore and Faery lore. Both involve lights that move in the sky, strange-looking creatures, nighttime encounters, kidnapping, and time displacement. Whatever this phenomenon is, it seems to have been around for a very long time. The explanation for it is always in accord with the technology of the period. In the Middle Ages the explanation was Faery activity, and in our contemporary era the explanation is extraterrestrial visitations. Centuries from now it will likely be something else.

My own view is that Faeries are beings who exist in another dimension, and who have interacted with humankind for countless centuries. They possess the ability/technology to move back and forth between their dimension and our own. I will admit to having personal experiences with the Faery race as I perceive them. Some of these meetings have been wonderful, and others were very disturbing. One particular encounter was actually quite unsettling in which a Faery took on the form of a frightening creature. A teacher of mine once said that if all our encounters with Faeries are always lovely ones, then we are not actually having any.

When I reflect upon my own encounters with Faeries, in comparison with reported Faery encounters in the time of the witchcraft trials, I cannot dismiss the reality of the latter. The reactions of the people, and their interpretation of events, do make sense to me (although I understand the experience differently). People in past periods thought and reacted in ways not unexpected for the time period in which they lived. Therefore, the reports of Faery encounters in the Middle Ages and Renaissance contain both grain and chaff. The same is true today.

I believe it is easier for people who have Faery encounters to arrive at a closer understanding of the events than it is for those who have not had their own personal experience. Likewise, I believe that people who practice witchcraft, and have had the experiences it can generate, are better able to sort the facts from the fantasy. From this perspective a modern witch's understanding about what appears in the writings on witchcraft in the past is based upon his or her experience in the world of witchcraft. The understanding of an inexperienced person will always fall short of fully grasping witches and witchcraft.

The type of witchcraft I refer to has little in common with popular modern notions about witchcraft. Old World witchcraft is glimpsed in shadow because the shadow's edge is the threshold of the portal to the inside. Stepping across the threshold and coming back again are what brings about realization. They reveal the difference between witchcraft as something to do on the weekend and witchcraft as something much larger and greater than the witch. Old World witchcraft is empowering and transformative. It is more than a philosophy and a self-image; it is how we interact with our connection to, and relationship with, all things.

There is a reason why witchcraft is traditionally linked to the night and intimately connected to the moon. In a mystical sense the moon is a *form* and is *formless* at the same time. From earth's perspective the moon appears to change shape in the night sky and even disappears entirely for three nights each lunar cycle. Its shape is not constant like that of the sun and stars. Therefore, it becomes a metaphor for altered states of consciousness. To stand beneath the moon in a state of receptivity is to invite the "other-world" into our mind, body, and spirit.

As humans we possess what is essentially a duality of *awareness*: conscious and subconscious. In Old World witchcraft the conscious mind is linked to the sun and the subconscious mind to the moon. We often call the conscious mind "the guardian," and it is his role to deal with material reality. He keeps us focused on the finite, tangible, and linear realities because they serve to sustain the life of the physical body. The subconscious mind is known as "the way-shower," and her role is to reveal nonmaterial reality. She keeps us connected to the limitless, ethereal, and spherical realities because they serve to sustain the spiritual nourishment of the soul. The conscious and subconscious minds are two equal halves of one greater whole; by analogy, we possess two arms, and it is more effective to use both than to always rely only upon one.

The guardian mind cannot, by itself, accept the existence of nonmaterial reality. In order to do so, it must share consciousness with the way-shower. For example, the guardian mind cannot believe in an invisible and silent deity because it does not experience this through the five senses. The way-shower has no objection to the idea of deity, but it cannot maintain it as a lasting concept (because in dreams nothing exists as something that cannot change form or meaning). It is only when the guardian and way-shower meet in a merged consciousness that *faith* becomes reality. Without this merged consciousness, the guardian regards faith as foundationless, and the way-shower sees it as merely a fading entertainment. But together our conscious and subconscious minds exchange part of their nature to each other. Through this exchange the conscious mind can accept *inexperienced* as something actualized, and the subconscious mind can regard *imagination* as a manifest and lasting form.

In Old World witchcraft the moon is not only a visible reminder of the occult mind; it is also the light that governs the most receptive time for a witch's magic—the night. Equally important is the fact that spirit activity is more pronounced at night. This is also the best time for communication with the dead. There is a difference between night and darkness. The former is determined through its relationship with the repeating cycle of light, and the latter is known by the shutting out of light. Therefore, we can be in night or in darkness. The Old World witch works with the night.

Folkloric sources indicate a belief that Faeries and witches have a fondness for dancing at night in the woods and meadows. Folktales mention flattened plants that form circles on the ground, which are said to be evidence of such dances. These spots are known as Faery-circles or hag-circles. The scientific explanation is that these are caused by the growth of fungi, which can grow in a circular pattern. This reminds me of an old belief that witches can cause the moon to excrete magical foam on the ground (said to be associated with calling down the moon from the night sky). Ancient writers such as Lucan refer to it as *virus lunare*, and witches were believed to gather it up to aid their enchantments. I was taught that this idea originated from a misunderstanding about the practice in witchcraft of wetting objects with the early morning dew that collects on lichen. Dew is heaviest on the morning following a full moon—enough said.

Returning to the theme of night gatherings, in chapter two we saw early references in the Christian era that mention the *tregenda*. This, we noted, was originally a gathering of witches involving formal communication with the dead. In Old World witchcraft the dead are intimately connected with the moon. Dancing with the dead at night is one of the features of the Sabbat, or tregenda. This involves making "birch dolls" fashioned with short birch twigs (roughly the length from the tip of the index finger on the left hand down to the wrist). The twigs are bound together with a cord. The cut ends are pushed into a pouch, which is then tied tightly with another cord. This forms a "head" on the doll, with

Birch Doll

the branches extending downward making the doll's body. These dolls represent the dead. During the dance, they are tossed back and forth through the air between the dancers.[53]

Ancient writers such as Plutarch wrote about the souls of the dead being drawn to the moon where they abide for a time and are later reborn on the earth. For us the circle of the moon in the night sky symbolizes the cycle of rebirth and the dwelling place of departed souls. Circle dances symbolically unite the living and the dead and keep alive the connection between past and present generations. One ancient belief held that the moon is literally a goddess (as opposed to a cult object associated with her). In this regard it is comforting to think of the womb of this goddess filled with the light of souls residing within her and awaiting rebirth (poetic though it may be).

In Old World witchcraft the trees are intimately connected with spirits of the dead. Old lore presents the idea that departed souls await rebirth in trees. Our lore associated with this idea involves an interesting concept that is said to be quite old. Souls are released from the full moon and come down into the woods where they pass into the trees. Looking at the full moon through the trees, their branches appear as though they touch her light. These limbs can be perceived as pathways or bridges that con-nect the world of the living to the realm of the dead.[54] A teach-ing once imparted to me described the belief that only certain trees are used as conduits to and from the Otherworld. These trees bear signs such as a hollow on the trunk (known as a Faery door) or some special mark that is suggestive of a face. It is not uncommon for these faces to resemble that of a creature from an old Faery tale. The teaching adds that in the Otherworld the counterpart trees have a *glimmer* about them, which points them out as passageways to the mortal world. In a discussion about this (with some fellow witches), the idea arose that these trees happen to stand at an intersection where the *fabric* of two different dimensions meet or overlap. Seeing them is like noticing a path into the woods or through the hills. Knowing where they are, and remembering how to find them again, takes a witch or a Faery, or so the old tales tell us.

Mystical ideas associated with trees make the body of a tree, and anything produced on the tree, useful as a tool of magic. The belief is that anything grown on the tree possesses the essence of the tree's nature (or spirit). This is one of the reasons why wands have been valued by witches for ages. They appear in some of the oldest literature about witches. Among the earliest mentions in Western literature are the beech, olive, and birch. Others follow in time and are regarded as being particularly potent. Oak and willow are two examples.

So far we've looked at a depiction of the Old Ways witch that presents her or his connection to mystical themes. But the witch is also a magician who works with the forces of the earth, the celestial and chthonic powers. In the next chapter we will fully explore the use of plants in witchcraft, but for now our examination will focus on the essence of magic itself.

In old witch lore, and in witchcraft trial transcripts, we find mentions of the use of roots, image-figures, potions, ointments, and various body parts of specific animals. The latter are most often nocturnal animals or amphibian creatures. As we noted, the night is intimately associated with witchcraft because of its lunar connection. Creatures such as the toad or frog are valued because they represent the power of transformation. This is due to their unique life cycle from the tadpole phase onward. These creatures are also totems of deities associated with witchcraft since ancient times. Lakes and ponds feature in old tales as entryways into the Otherworld or Underworld. Therefore, it is no surprise to find creatures that can pass back and forth from bodies of water to be linked to magic. In effect they live in both worlds (the seen and the unseen) and are therefore agents of magic.

To understand why things are used in magic, we need to recognize an old teaching. From an occult view anything that is previously part of something will always maintain a connection to it. This belief is the root of the magical idea of using a person's hair or fingernail clippings to cast a spell on her or him. This is what I sometimes refer to as the "*leapfrog*" principle of primitive magic; however, the series of *lily pads* or *stepping-stones* in this analogy leads to other connections as well.

The idea of leapfrog magic is to reach one point through a series of connecting ones. The points generate communication to and from each other, and this can flow in the form of magical energy. One example is the toad. Why would someone want to use this creature in a magical sense? The answer is that the toad is connected to the real source of power that a witch wants to tap. It is not the toad; it is what can come from the links leading to the toad. The creature is simply what we can touch or hold in the material world, but what the witch seeks is that which can be attracted through contact with the toad. This does not reside in the flesh of the toad; it comes from nonmaterial reality directly linked to the toad. These links were fashioned long ago by witchcraft practitioners, and this is very old magic we are dealing with here.

Images of toads or frogs appear in prehistoric times in the form of carved and painted figures. They often seem to be symbols of fertility and birth. Anthropologist Marija Gimbutas points to the frog or toad as symbolic of a goddess associated with death and regeneration. She also links the creature to the ancient belief in a "wandering womb" found in Egyptian and classical sources.[55] The frog or toad is associated with the goddess Hecate who was a Titan, which links her with a prehistoric race of deities.[56]

One form of magic involving the frog or toad is the belief in a key-shaped bone inside the body. To possess the key-bone granted one special powers (and the powers vary according to regional folkloric beliefs). Whatever the case may be, the symbol of the key can be linked to Hecate. She is the source of power at the end of the backward leap-frog journey from the frog or toad. One of her aspects is the guardian of portals and gateways. She is also intimately connected to the Underworld and to the crossroads.

In witchcraft, bones are used to contact spirits, especially those of the dead. Objects like the frog-bone can be left at the crossroads overnight in the belief that a Faery rider may take it. In old lore, Faeries ride on white horses, and if one makes off with the bone, it takes its Otherworld counterpart and leaves behind the material bone. Because links remain between objects previously connected, the physical bone possesses power through its Faery Realm connection. A related belief holds that the frog-bone grants its possessor power over horses. Here we see a connection back to the Faery rider and the white horse.

In the literary tradition of witchcraft tales, the witch does not generate power from within herself. She calls upon external things that release their power to her, which she can then direct. The writings of this period are in keeping with associated beliefs that objects possess a type of consciousness, or force, known as *numen*. In other cultures this is known as *mana*. The witch communicates with objects, and they transfer some of their energy to her or him.

As the centuries pass, the idea of the witch's power changes with time. In the Christian era we find traces of a belief that the witch herself has internal power. This power is either inherited or passed through an object. The latter can be a charm, a piece of parchment, a book, or a familiar spirit. Eventually, the belief is distorted, and the power of a witch becomes attached to a pact with the Devil.

The introduction of the Devil is an interesting event, and the question must be asked—did witches involve themselves with him? But the more important question is how did witches perceive the Devil? Witches in the Christian era certainly knew about this character because it contaminated the views of all social classes. Was he a distorted form of a pagan god? Or was he a new figure that arrived in the witchcraft scene?

In her book, *By-Paths in Sicily*, author Eliza Heaton presents an interesting view of the Devil in folk magic circa 1920. Heaton describes various personal encounters with a woman named Vanna, whom many people might call a witch, but she refers to herself as a Christian. In her hair Vanna wears what are called elf-locks. This is a very long braid that marks her as a person trained by Faeries. In Heaton's book there is a fascinating report of Faery encounters that Vanna relates from childhood days.

One day Heaton asks Vanna why her incantations often include calling upon the Devil. Vanna replies, "He has great power," and apparently she sees no conflict in including him in her magic.[57] In the book it is clear that Vanna thinks of the Devil in keeping with the stereotypical depiction. This is an interesting view of working with the Devil while not venerating him, making a pact, or accepting him as a personal master.

The Devil, of course, is not a pre-Christian European entity. He is imported into Europe from the Middle East and therefore has no original place in the Old World witchcraft of Europe as I know it. However, because the Church used the imagery of pre-Christian deity forms to depict the Devil (and demons), it becomes difficult to completely divorce an association with witchcraft. Confused peasants may have viewed the Devil as one of the old gods seen in a distorted way by the Church and its operatives. If Old World witches ever called upon this entity, it was not the Devil of Judeo-Christian culture. It was instead the pre-Christian represented imagery of horn and hoof in which they recognized power.[58]

When considering the history of the Devil's appearance in writings about witchcraft, we cannot avoid references to Lucifer. In chapter two we noted him, but we must now go deeper in our exploration. In contemporary witchcraft we find two main streams of ideas flowing into modern views. One idea is related to the figure known as Cain, and the other to Lucifer. Both appear to bring elements of Judeo-Christian lore along with them (reinterpreted though they may be). Both of these streams also carry bits of lore from the concept of Lilith as she appears in an unofficial myth attached to the Garden of Eden story. Here she is the first wife made for Adam, who rejects her because she behaves as his equal. As a result, God banishes her and then creates Eve from a rib lifted from Adam's side, which denotes partnership to a lesser degree. In other words, Eve is subordinate to Adam in the Eden mythos.

Theologians, such as St. Augustine, put forth the notion that the descendants of Cain are inherently evil.[59] Historian Montague Summers, in his book *Witchcraft and Black Magic*, tries to trace witchcraft from a revival in the time of Noah. Summers states that Ham revived the ways of witchcraft (after the Great Flood) and initiated his son Mizraim into its mysteries. But there is no mention of how Cain's bloodline survived the Flood (for Ham was Noah's son, himself directly descended from Adam). For Cain's direct line to have lasted, one of the son's wives on the Ark would have to be a descendant of Cain.

In a Jewish extra-biblical tradition related to the Flood story, Noah allows Og (a son of Ham's wife) to save himself by clinging to the outside of the Ark. In one version of the tale Og is a giant, perhaps one of the Nephilim. The Nephilim appear in the Book of Genesis (6:1–4) and seem to be associated with the "sons of god" (angels) who mate with human women and produce offspring. The children of these angels and mortals are referred to as "the mighty men that were of old, the men of renown." The biblical verse states the Nephilim appear on earth after the mating between the sons of god and women. In popular belief the Nephilim are the offspring of this union, but this does not seem to agree with the chronology of events in the biblical account. References to the Nephilim appear later in Numbers 13:33 where they are referred to as the Anakim, the descendants of Anak (who in old lore is sometimes referred to as the first witch).

Summers argues that Ham studied the teachings of the fallen angels mentioned in the Book of Enoch as the Watchers. Ham also bore the name Ham-Zoroaster, which is possibly an attempt to connect him with the stellar cults of the Chaldeans/Babylonians. As mentioned, Ham initiated Mizraim (who reportedly left a legacy of magic to the Egyptians and other regions).

Lucifer was originally associated with the planet Venus in Roman times, which in this era was perceived as the morning star.

In mythology he prepared the horses that carried the chariot of the sun through the day sky. In Latin his name means "the light-bringer," which is reflected in his mythological role related to the sun. In addition, Lucifer was the "herald of the light" because the appearance of Venus on the horizon is followed by the rising of the sun.

The Church concocted a connection between Satan and Lucifer through its misuse of a verse from the Book of Isaiah. In chapter 14, verses 12–15, the fall of the mighty king of Babylon is depicted. To the Hebrews of the period this king symbolized evil. The Hebrew word appearing in the reference in Isaiah is *Helel ben-shahar*, which means "bright son of the morning." The translators of the King James Bible inserted the Latin word Lucifer to take its place. This may have been the result of a New Testament verse in the Gospel of Luke (10:18), which refers to the fall of Satan from the heaven. Translators saw this reference to the fall of the king of Babylon as a metaphor, and so Satan became equated with Helel ben-shahar. The conflation between this name and Lucifer left the latter embedded in the persona of the Devil.

By the period of the Middle Ages, heretical sects existed that worshipped the Judeo-Christian devil under the name of Lucifer. As noted in earlier chapters, the Church was later successful in inventing a connection between witches and Satan. In this way, Lucifer became a name that appeared in the witchcraft trials. If indeed witches ever worshipped Lucifer, which one was it—the Judeo-Christian *Prince of Darkness* or the god known as the *Light-Bringer* in ancient Rome?

Folklorist Charles Leland published a "Gospel of the Witches" in the late nineteenth century that included Lucifer as the brother of Diana. In the book Leland also makes references to Cain, who is conjured at the Sabbat meal in Leland's text. Both Lucifer and Cain, in Leland's book, conform to the essential Judeo-Christian depictions that vilify them. Leland describes Lucifer as "the god of the Sun and of the Moon, the god of Light (*Splendor*), who was so proud of his beauty, and who for his pride was driven from Paradise."[60] Cain is also a figure driven from Paradise, and in old lore is said to be imprisoned on the moon. We previously noted the ancient Greek idea that souls are drawn into the sphere of the moon and then later released into rebirth on the earth. In this light it seems that Cain's punishment is to never reincarnate. This leaves him to forever be who he was in life.

On a side note we must look at the anti-Jewish sentiment in the Middle Ages and the anti-witch feelings of the same period. Transferring Old Testament figures such as Cain and Herodias into European witchcraft seems like an attempt to kill two birds with one stone. This contamination of witchcraft worked very well in tandem with the goals of heresy accusations. Satan was the cherry-on-top, and the formation of Judeo-Christian themes within witchcraft was complete.

In Old World witchcraft there is no embracing of Lucifer, Cain, or Herodias as any connective lineage. These currents (or threads connecting them) may appear in what is often called "traditional witchcraft" and certainly do appear in modern Luciferian witch-craft. The latter is often steeped in imagery reminiscent of the Church's historic depiction of diabolical witchcraft. In contrast with traditional witchcraft and Luciferian witchcraft, Old World witchcraft does not share any roots to Old Testament or New Testament connections with witchcraft (real or imagined). Likewise, it is not connected to any angelic lore such as the "fallen angels" or the Watchers mentioned in the Book of Enoch.

In order to sort out the differences between popular Neo-Pagan views of modern witches and Old Ways witches, we must reveal some important tenets. In the modern idea of Wicca as the religion of witches, we find the concept of its membership involved in an earth religion.[61] In other words, these are witches who venerate nature in some manner. Here we find the related idea of the earth as sentient, a goddess often called Gaia.

Old World witchcraft is not a nature religion as envisioned by the Neo-Pagan movement. It is also not a system solely devoted to magic. Witches appreciate and care for nature because they are part of nature. It sustains them, and they must sustain nature in return. In addition, nature provides witches with the plants of their craft and with materials for their ritual and magical tools. Therefore, witches honor their relationship with nature, but this relationship has much deeper levels than stated here.

Witches of the Old Ways draw power from the Hallow.[62] This is a term for the deep center of the forest where primal sacredness exists. From this center, power emanates outward to the three realms: above, below, and in-between. Power also flows into the Hallow from these realms as well. For modern practitioners this is a concept rather than an actual area in a forest, but the ancient practice of venerating a specific tree in a sacred grove is connected to the theme of the Hallow. In chapters four and five we will encounter the mortar and pestle, a magical tool representing direct connection to, and communication with, the Hallow.

Unlike most modern witchcraft traditions (or systems), the tools used in Old World witchcraft are relatively few by comparison. The classical "four ritual tools of Western occultism" are not incorporated in the same manner as in Wiccan tradition. In other words, the pentacle, wand, dagger, and chalice are not primary tools. The main tool of the Old Ways witch is the mortar and pestle. The broom and the cauldron are important tools, as is the ritual dagger. The wand is among the oldest of the witches' tools mentioned in the literary tradition, and it has special uses in Old World witchcraft. All of this is presented in the second half of the book, which contains a grimoire of Old World witchery.

Returning to the idea of a connection to nature, we must note the teachings associated with the sacredness of land, or more correctly, with the spirit of the land. It is an Old Ways teaching that certain areas possess a special nature because of the events that took place upon them. Some obvious examples are those places marked by "standing stones" and other prehistoric monuments, but places connected to death or dying also possess power. This is one of the reasons why cemeteries are featured in old witchcraft traditions.

One of the old beliefs is that spirits of the dead pass into inanimate objects at some point during the transition of the death experience. Markers are set to indicate the place of death and can serve as an interfacing mechanism (to use modern terminology). This principle was once part of the tradition of sanctifying the places where great heroes died or were buried. Such places were regarded as special zones of occult power. Today the presence of headstones in a cemetery reflects the idea of marking places where the dead lie. The ancient practice of laying offerings at "spirit places" seems now extended to placing flowers on a grave site.

Cemeteries and crossroads are often thought of as a place between the world of the living and the dead. In this light, they are access points to nonmaterial reality. But do the dead actually reside in such places, and if so, how does this reconcile with the idea of reincarnation? To better understand this we need to examine the old teachings. In them we find the belief that the soul enters into each incarnation and dons a persona known as the personality. By analogy, we wear selected clothing when we are at work, or at a formal occasion, and in this light, the soul wears a personality in each physical life. This personality is associated with the physical person in each life, but it is not the soul. The soul is the accumulated experiences of all the personalities it has worn throughout all of its incarnations.

According to the teachings, the personality, its sentient composition, does not continue on with the soul. It is instead absorbed into the "ancestral spirit," where it joins the hive mind and becomes one of the ancestors. The soul retains the life experience and memory of each personality but sheds its sentient connection. This is similar to the idea that at any given age a person is the accumulation of all the experiences she or he has to date. But the woman or man at age twenty-five is not the six-year-old or sixteen-year-old person they once were. However, the experiences of those past personalities have left an imprint.

In accord with the teachings, when we communicate with the dead we are connecting with the ancestral spirit. An exception is someone who has recently died and therefore has not yet joined the ancestors. In rare cases a personality can become bound to a place because of the person's death experience. It simply cannot move on or refuses to leave. This results in certain types of haunting phenomena.

In most cases, after death the soul reenters the cycle of rebirth, and the personality is separated (and enters its own realm). In Old World witchcraft we do not find the concept of the Summerland of Wiccan belief. Instead, the soul is believed to enter the sphere of the moon (represented by the physical moon). In modern terminology this refers to a process more than a place. However, it is still taught that the sphere of the moon (sometimes called the realm of Luna) is a spirit world in which reincarnating souls await rebirth into bodies of flesh.

Another teaching associated with departed souls is related to the Faery Realm. This reflects a very old belief that after death we can enter this realm and become Faeries. Such a belief appears in early forms of lore. One example appears in the writings of folklorist Christine Messina. She points out that in the early tale of Cinderella her "Fairy God Mother" is actually the spirit of her dead mother come from the Faery Realm to render aid.[63] The mother manifests from a small tree gifted by a fairy woman at the Grotto of the Faeries. In similar ways, the wooden puppet Pinocchio is given life by the Blue Faery who is the departed wife of Gipetto (and with whom he never had a child before she died).

In the following chapters we will explore other beliefs and practices rooted in the Old World or Enchanted World view, but for now let us look at a formal system constructed around the beliefs and practices of Old World witchcraft. It is known as Ash, Birch, and Willow. This will provide an example of how the old and new can come together in a way that does justice to both. We must note that this system is just one of many ways in which to incorporate elements of Old World witchcraft into a structured modern system of ritual practice.

Ash, Birch, and Willow

In order not to misunderstand the system of Ash, Birch, and Willow (ABW), we must note something up front. ABW is witchcraft as a religion that includes a magical system with its structure. It incorporates elements of Neo-Paganism along with older models. The system does include seasonal rites reminiscent of the eight Sabbats in modern Wicca. However, the rituals are somewhat different and work with depths related to the ancient mystery traditions. The rituals of ABW are rooted specifically in the inner mysteries reflected in the seed cycle: seed, stem, leaf, bud, flower, and fruit. This cycle is viewed as a metaphor for the journey of the soul through reincarnation.

In keeping with the connection of witches to the plant kingdom, the system of ABW incorporates the agricultural seasons into the festivals of the year. This is a modern structure based upon ancient festivals that once marked the important times of planting and harvesting. The midpoints between each solstice and equinox are included as well, for they mark magical times that flow in and out of the four major agricultural periods. The celebrating of the seasons is the spiritual connection to the land and the divine emanation that is associated with these key tides in nature.

In essence Ash, Birch, and Willow is a training system rooted in the initiatory teachings and understandings of Old World witchcraft. Its goal is to provide the inner teachings and ritual experience that were once available only within secret societies. I first conceived of ABW along with author Stephanie Taylor in 2004. It is based upon the ancient beliefs and practices of Old World Europe and is adapted to the needs of a modern generation. Therefore, the system has appeal to anyone with an appreciation of rooted traditions and contemporary applications.

Within Ash, Birch, and Willow, there is a degree system of three levels. The name of the system is based upon old lore associated with ash, birch, and willow trees. These are the three woods traditionally used to make a witch's broom. The handle is made of ash, the sweep is birch, and strips of willow bark are used to lash them together. Metaphorically speaking, the witch's broom allows the witch to fly through the sky; the teachings of ABW enable the witch to soar within the inner planes and mystical realms.

Traditionally, the ash encompasses the Three Worlds of ancient myth and legend: Overworld, Middleworld, and Underworld. Birch traditionally is a protection when working with Otherworld beings. On the witches' broom, the birch grants power to direct spirits of the Otherworld, and therefore allows for safe passage. Willow is sacred to the goddess Hecate, who has long been associated with witchcraft. In ancient myth, Hecate ruled over the three known worlds and, as such, was the Great Goddess of the great realms. The willow strips represent the binding oath of initiation. The broom, as a complete symbol, represents all of these inner connections that empower the witch. In effect, it proclaims the witch as one who traverses other realities and is empowered by the goddess of magic and witchcraft.

The format of ABW is representative of the commonality of European paganism. Therefore, it is not restricted to any specific cultural tradition such as Celtic, Germanic, French, Italian, or Greek. Instead, the tradition reflects the core beliefs and practices of all. In order to reflect the commonality of European pagan concepts from various regions, the tradition uses titles for the Goddess and God. These titles express the nature of the goddess and god as reflected in the seasons of the year. Modern practitioners work with a goddess and god figure, but in the older views these entities are more like spirits or sentient forces.

In the ABW system we most often use titles for the deities. These appear in the "Wheel of the Year" celebrations, which are a newer practice not found collectively in the earlier practices of witchcraft. Most Wiccan systems use the Wheel of the Year, and some people regard its presence anywhere as definitive of Wicca.

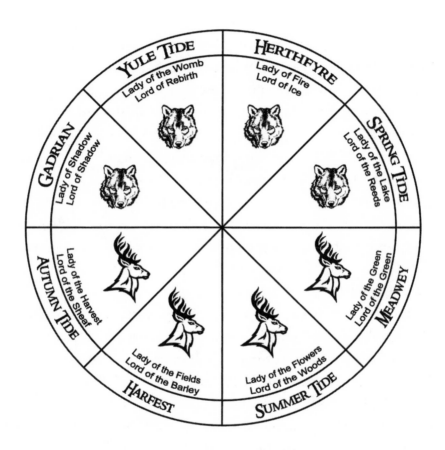

However, Old Ways witches do not think of the concept of the Wheel as being trademarked by any specific path. It is now simply part of Neo-Pagan practices, and there is nothing wrong with sharing it as a template to create annual festival celebrations.

The ABW year begins on November Eve, and its festival name is Gadrian, which is an old word meaning *gathering*. At this time we call upon the Lady of Shadow and Lord of Shadow. In a metaphysical sense, shadow is the manifested form of that which cannot be directly seen. In other words, the original image withholds the light in which it is completely visible and the blocked light produces a resembling image. A mundane example is the casting of hand-shadows on a wall. What we see is a projected image that resembles a hand but is a poor copy that lacks the details. In the case of the "Lady" and "Lord," what we see in shadow are forms of potentiality that suggest a greater force behind them. The time of shadow is a call to begin the journey to the light that dissolves away illusionary projections.

At the season of Yule Tide, we use the titles Lady of the Womb and Lord of Rebirth. These titles reflect a process (rebirth) and the vessel through which it manifests (the womb). These are very old concepts, and in prehistoric art we find the depiction of the female body in many themes of generation/regeneration. Yule reminds us that the portals to and from the worlds can be accessed through the Womb Gate. The vitalizing light of the Otherworld is accessible in our journey where it imbues the soul, just as the light of the sun is sensory to the body in the material realm.

With the season of Herthfyre (on February Eve), the titles "Lady of Fire" and "Lord of Ice" appear. The seeds of life are frozen and stilled beneath the wintered land. It is the transforming passion of the Lady of Fire that arouses the seed to rise and penetrate into the realm of light. At this season, we are reminded that even in the greatest times of restriction and confinement, we must never resist the fire that calls us to growth and expansion. It is this fire that purifies us for the spiritual journey ahead. Things around us may try to impose restriction, but they have no true power over the light (other than what we allow).

For the season of Spring Tide, we use the titles Lady of the Lake and Lord of the Reeds. The winter thaws, and the waters return to their former state. Life is renewed as seeds and roots respond to warmth and moisture. The season reminds us that the light calls us from the depths back to the surface where we begin anew. Yet each time carries the experience of the former cycle, and through this the parts become the whole.

At the celebration of Meadwey (on May Eve), we use the titles Lady of the Green and Lord of the Green. The new vessels and bearers of the seed come into their time of power. The season reminds us of the tenacity of life and therefore of the light itself. Forms may change but the cycle does not, and by nature's reflection of the divine mechanism, we are assured of our own renewal and return.

With the arrival of Summer Tide, the titles become Lady of the Flowers and Lord of the Woods. Buds and blossoms form on the plants in sunlight and in shade. We are reminded that life and death are but two parts of a greater whole. The legend of the Mid-Summer gathering of Faeries takes on new meaning at this pivotal moment between life and pending death (as reflected in the waxing and waning seasons). Light and shadow begin their annual dance that generates the ever-turning Wheel of the Year.

When the August Eve festival of Harfest arrives, we turn to using the titles Lady of the Fields and Lord of the Barley. The time of harvest, or a pending harvest, is upon us as nature's bounty surrounds us. Here we see the whole (fields) in relationship to its parts (barley plants). They need to be separated and yet must be reunited again. Through this we are reminded that our souls must separate from matter, renew themselves in spirit, and become the seeds of light that generate a new incarnation.

At the time of Autumn Tide, we use the titles Lady of the Harvest and Lord of the Sheaf. The stalks are cut and gathered together. Chaff and grain are sorted; the grain is kept safe to renew life in the spring. In this season we are reminded that it is the essence that survives even when the seed-bearing vessel dies. The light of the soul is the seed that is kept safe after death of the body. In its time it will enter the earth and awaken in a new season of the divine cycle of birth, life, death, and renewal.

The Wheel of the Year in ABW is intended to honor the spirit of pre-Christian ways within a modern blend of European traditions. ABW is not a reconstruction or modern interpretation. Instead, it is an integration of the spirit of the pre-Christian people into a contemporary format. Its parts include ancient themes and lore associated with hunting and farming. These touch the animal and plant realms, which in turn place their ancient lore into our hands and hearts. While ABW does claim a spiritual lineage to ancient times, it does not profess to be the descendant of any former cohesive tradition.

Like many modern systems, ABW uses a ritual circle and an altar. The circle marks out the boundaries of the ritual and magic area, and it represents the full moon drawn upon the ground. This evokes the occult principle of "as above, so below" and joins the earthly and lunar realms together. The altar marks the direct center of the circle and becomes the directing spiritual force for each rite. Like most modern systems of witchcraft, the elemental forces are used to create and maintain the circle. When the ritual is completed, the elemental forces are released to return to their natural realms.

A ritual circle in the ABW system is connected not only to the lunar realm but also to the plant kingdom. This is one of the reasons herbs are sprinkled along the edge of the circle, covering the entire perimeter. This is comprised of rue, vervain, and Saint-John's-wort. Old lore tells that this is a powerful combination against harmful influences and entities.

Throughout this chapter we have looked at the witch figure through the lens of old beliefs, legends, and lore. In the text that follows the witch is further revealed in her or his nature as one intimately connected to the plant kingdom. Let us move through the thicket and examine the witch in the enchanted world of magical plants and herbs.

Chapter Four

WITCHES:
THE PLANT PEOPLE

Earlier we encountered the idea of witches as "the plant people" in ancient times. As previously noted the word *pharmakis*
is the earliest to denote a witch in Western culture. Here we
will further explore this theme and look at the relationship of
the witch and the traditional plants of witchcraft. This will lead
us into the realm of chthonic spirits and entities of night and
shadow.

The traditional plants of witchcraft are well known, as is their
legendary lore. They include the *mandrake, hemlock, henbane,
foxglove, belladonna, aconite,* and *wolf's bane* plant. Each of these
plants is poisonous and can be quite deadly if used incorrectly.
Unfortunately, the old lore is contaminated by the intentional
portrayal of witches as evil people who use poison to harm others.
While it is true that the knowledge of poison exists in Old World
witchcraft, the reason for this is not one of causing physical harm.
I was taught that to know the healing properties of plants we must
also know the harmful levels. Likewise, in order to know what
levels safely alter consciousness, we must also understand what

levels are lethal. The balanced application of such knowledge has long been part of the witches' craft.

In Old World witchcraft, plants are part of a spiritual tradition, which is sometimes referred to as the Green Wisdom. This is a modern view in terms of phraseology, but it is not one in discord with ancient thought. People in the past believed that specific spirits felt a connection to, or had an affinity with, specific plants. This drew the spirit to the plant. The basic philosophy of affinity or connection lies behind the tradition of occult correspondences, which include the association of plants and minerals with planetary or magical natures.

In the sense of *spiritual botany*, a plant is divided into symbolic sections that create correspondences to a magical nature:

> Root: command, control, and bind
>
> Crown: transition and connecting opposites
>
> Stem/Trunk: changing perspectives and new insights
>
> Leaves: empowering and energizing
>
> Bud: opportunities and potential
>
> Flower: spiritual connections
>
> Fruit: completion and reflection
>
> Seed: continuation and preservation

These correspondences can be applied when planning how to use a plant for a specific magical intent. One or more correspondences conforming to the magical intention can be added to a spell, which then calls for using additional parts of the plant. The goal is to add specific plant powers to charge the spell. Bear in mind that various plants possess their own spirit, and therefore, the parts of these plants will accordingly influence the correspondence in some way. Chapter five covers this in the grimoire section.

The idea of "spiritual botany" is rooted in the concept that the Green World is inhabited by spirits whose power is passed to plants. This is tied to the magical principle that objects in close proximity exchange, or share, their natures. Here the plant takes on a portion of the spirit's nature and vice versa. In some systems this energy is called *shadow*, and from this comes the magical concept of *sharing shadow* (passing power). As it relates to plants, shadow is the mystical force drawn into the plant from beneath the surface of the soil. This is known as the hidden realm, a term that is also connected to the idea of the realm of the dead. There are mystical forces that reside in the mineral material of the earth, and the roots of plants tap into them. The spirits linked to the plant world also access them.

Connected to the concept of sharing shadow is the idea of the spirit of the land. This is reflected in early beliefs that specific areas of land are home to primal spirits. These beings are sometimes called the *genius loci*, or *genii loci*, and are in essence the spirit of a place. In archaic religion they were guardian spirits or tutelary deities. We often sense their presence in the "feeling" of a place. Various things can adversely affect this feeling, including events taking place on a battlefield or heinous crimes committed in a specific area. Positive influences can also set into the land such as the existence of a temple or the site of joyous celebrations, or festivals taking place over time. The spirits of a place *remember* all these things.

At times the genii loci communicate to humans by causing a leaf or some other part of a plant to appear to have a face. This is performed in recognition of the human presence and is a response to her or his presence. Whenever it takes place, this is a moment in which interfacing is possible (and usually welcomed). The degree to which this is extended is reflected in the type of face shown. Does it appear friendly, mischievous, challenging, or playful? Gently press a leaf from a tree to your face (without harming the leaf) and impart your positive feelings about nature into it. Next, carefully turn the leaf to face the object showing the genii loci's resemblance of a face. Gently blow across the leaf with the feeling that your energy is transmitted to the spirit. This action on your part is a sign of peace, and your goodwill is thereby conveyed to the forest. This will make your encounter much more beneficial.

All plants also possess what is often called the *genius*. This is the plant's conscious connection to the Group Mind of the Green World. Through this connection a plant holds the memory of its species throughout time. It is, in effect, the spiritual DNA of the plant. Through an established connection and rapport with the plant's genius, the witch can summon the greater forces of Green Magic. The genius will share its shadow with you if shown the proper respect and protocol.

In addition to herbs, we find a variety of trees included in Old Ways witchcraft. The list includes the hawthorn, blackthorn, rowan, myrtle, walnut, ash, birch, and willow. Some of these appear in folk traditions as trees that protect against witchcraft. In such accounts we need to remember that most often the word "enchantment" has been replaced by the word "witchcraft." As noted in other chapters, witches utilize protection against magic/enchantment just as do all magic-users in one way or another. Therefore, we need to be careful in labeling anti-magic or counter-magic items and methods as protection specifically against witchcraft.

In Old Ways witchcraft, the forest is viewed as self-aware and conscious of the world. It draws things into itself, dissolves, integrates, and then regenerates them. This inner mechanism is connected to what is called the Hallow. As noted in chapter three, the Hallow draws the three realms (above, below, and in-between) together in such a way that power and communication freely flow between them. This concept is illustrated by the image of a mystical tree with its branches in the Overworld, its trunk in the Middleworld, and its roots in the Underworld.

The branches of the trees, when seen against the sun and moon, are regarded mystically as pathways leading to and from the sun and moon (through a magical or spiritual perspective). It is believed that spirits travel across these networks, bridges, or pathways. Communication in the form of prayers or incantations flows along them as well. This is one of the reasons a branch in the form of a stang or a wand is valued in the art of Old Ways witchcraft.

As noted in chapter three, an ancient belief, spoken about by such figures as Plutarch, holds that the moon is the abode of the dead.[64] According to such beliefs, departed souls are drawn into the moon where they remain until they are released back into new mortal bodies. In earlier chapters we noted that witches have long been associated with the dead and with the moon. Among the oldest references to witchcraft is the gathering of witches at the crossroads, which was the place where wandering spirits of the dead were said to gather. Hecate, the goddess of witchcraft, ruled over the crossroads and was associated with the souls of the dead. In some tales she is said to lead a train of wandering souls in the night sky.

Plutarch mentions ancient beliefs about tree veneration that connects to spirits of the dead. These include a tenet that the souls of heroes and "the virtuous dead" continue life in the trees. Another belief is that souls reincarnate through trees, which connects with the precept that souls ascend into the heaven world through holes in the canopy.[65] Such ideologies harmonize with the concept in Old World witchcraft that spirits travel through the pathways of the forest branches that "touch" the moon. In modern times we view all of this as a poetic metaphor, but Old Ways witches acknowledge a time when such beliefs simply reflected the way of things. We will revisit this theme later in the section on the lore of the White Tree.

In ancient times the idea that spirits inhabit plants was a very strong belief. This is also an old shamanic belief, and intoxication experienced by ingesting plants or their substances is regarded as a type of spirit possession. In the ancient rites of Dionysus, wine was consumed to produce intoxication in the belief that an altered state of consciousness is caused by the spirit of Dionysus entering into the flesh body. In magical terms everything physical has a metaphysical counterpart. In science what is referred to as the pharmaceutical properties of a plant is, in metaphysics, the intrinsic nature of the plant that allows its spirit to merge with us in the flesh. It is the internal mystical mechanism.

In the early days of my occult training, I was taught that certain spirits have an attraction to specific plants. They are involved in the development of the plant's properties and inhabit the material body of the plant in a manner similar to the idea of the soul dwelling in a human body. For magical purposes the spirit can be persuaded to extend its influence to a removed part of the plant such as a root or some of its leaves. In some cases a complete transference of the spirit is possible, but to take the life of the entire plant without consulting the indwelling spirit is entirely another matter (because it forces the spirit from its abode). It is not wise for the witch to have such a reputation in the spirit world.

It is important to the success of working with plants and their spirits for the witch to gain a rapport. Ideally, this should begin with the seed and continue as the plant emerges and grows to fullness. A rapport can be created at almost any phase of the plant's growth, but the longer a relationship exists between you and the plant, the stronger will be the rapport.

Using the veins in the leaves of the plant heightens communication with the plant and its spirit. Begin by lightly tracing the veins with your fingertips, starting at the tip of the leaf and working toward the stem. As you touch the plant, communicate with it through word or by focusing your thoughts. Introduce yourself as a witch by saying that you are one of the *pharmaceute* (pronounced far-mah-koo-tay). This is a sharing of spiritual lineage that connects you to the plant, which then moves the plant to share its magical lineage with you. This rapport with the plant encourages it to share shadow with you.

When physically connecting with the plant, tell it you will care for and protect it as it grows. Let the plant know its assigned magical nature and give it some examples of what its power can accomplish. This is a magical technique known as *informing*. The instructions you transmit will help tune the plant to your magical intentions and will connect you with the consciousness of the spirit dwelling in the plant. For example, you can inform a belladonna plant that it possesses the ability to stir passion in human emotions. Other examples and uses can be found in the grimoire section of chapter five in this book. You can create deeper levels of connection to the magical intent passed to a plant by using magically charged water. Water eventually becomes the *green blood* of the plant, which spreads the magical intent to all parts of the plant. Using a table of magical correspondences, you can imbue the plant with an elemental nature to enhance its power. For example, elemental earth can be used to shield or bind, air to transmit ideas to other minds, fire to cause the transformation of one state to another, and water to cleanse and create movement (see the grimoire for complete correspondences). Think about which element can enhance the power of a plant, and then pass that element to it through water. This is accomplished by evoking the elemental energies and directing them into the water (see the grimoire for instructions about charging with elemental forces).

Witches, as people of the plants, possess a connection to the material aspect of a plant, its inherent properties, and its familiar spirit. Each plant has a triple nature, which is true of most things in the magical realm. The roots of a plant connect it to the Underworld (spirit realm), its leaves to the Overworld (celestial nature), and the seeds to the Middleworld (the material dimension). In most cases all three realms are called into play for the purposes of casting a spell or using the plant for some specific purpose. One example is using an ivy plant to bind someone from harming others. In this case, the leaves (with stem) bind the spirit of the predator (her or his drive or desire). The roots drain off the power of the person, and the seeds are crushed to cease future attacks.

In Old Ways witchcraft a witch must establish specific connections with the plant kingdom. The first and strongest connection involves obtaining a mandrake root. This is sometimes known as the sorcerer's root and is placed in a pouch that is worn on the body. Possession of the mandrake is a sign of mastery of the magical arts of witchcraft; the spirits of the plant world take serious note of its presence in the hands of a witch.

Because the witch knows the triple nature, she or he then creates a connection with the powers of night and day.[66] The plant kingdom is greatly affected by the cycle of light, and therefore its indwelling spirits are as well. Magical tools are used to direct these spirits, which includes calling them and bidding them farewell. The specific tools used for such purposes are the white thorn wand (hawthorn) and the black thorn wand. Ideally, these should be fashioned into canes or walking sticks.

Once in hand, these wands are used to direct magical charges to and from informed plants. The wands also evoke the familiar spirit within a plant. Blackthorn is associated with the powers of the night, and hawthorn with those of the day. Both of these wands are defensive and offensive in the art of magical combat. Anyone who works with the powers generated through witchcraft will need both skills.

The white thorn (hawthorn) and black thorn have Faery connections in old lore. This ties in with the teaching that sometimes Faeries pass on the secret knowledge of plants and plant spirits to mortals. The associated magic, as we understand it, emanates from the Faery Realm. This is perceived as the *glimmer*, a type of light that can influence boundaries and material things (as well as living beings). In the Faery Realm something emanating glimmer can serve as a portal between dimensions. It also produces effects that humans interpret as the experience of altered time.

Faery teachings include the idea that spirits impart something of their nature into plants, particularly into their roots. It is the root of the plant where life is sustained, and from the root all parts of the plant receive what is needed. One misunderstanding about the root lies in a Christian era belief that a mandrake root has the power to overcome light and is therefore an agent of darkness. This belief connected the mandrake to the activities of demons.

In Old Ways witchcraft the mandrake root has the ability to evoke the procreative state, which is associated with the black of night. In this regard it magically returns something to its pre-manifest state, and from within this setting of complete potentiality, re-creation or renewal can take place as directed by the witch. So it is not that the mandrake conquers or banishes light, but in contrast it has the power to restore the blackness of procreation from which all things issue forth into the world of light.

Knowing the Spirits

In this section we will look at a variety of important plants, their properties, and the spirits associated with them. Working with spirits of the plants is an effective way of maintaining access to the Greenwood Magic. Once a rapport is established, it is possible to draw upon the magical nature of plants even when they are not physically available to you. It is for times like this that you can use "spirit seals" to evoke or invoke the magical nature of a plant. These seals connect with astral keys that open communication. In essence, they are bridges between you and shadow.

Names are given to the spirit of each plant through which contact can be made. The use of a name is a means of communication and serves as a stimulating energy. To speak the name of a plant draws its attention and places you and plant together so that both are fully present in the moment.

Because of the serious danger of working with poisonous and hallucinogenic plants, I am not encouraging you to obtain them or come into contact with them. But in order that you may still work with the spirits of these plants, I have devised a magical system that uses magical seals. These plant-spirit seals can be found in chapter five's grimoire section, but for now, let us meet the Old Ways spirits.

Mandrake is the primary plant of the Old Ways witch. Because its root takes the shape of a human, it is the magical nexus. The mandrake root represents the material existence of mortals, the earthly roots that hold their souls on earth. The root is also the abode of chthonic spirits who are likewise drawn to a form of material existence.

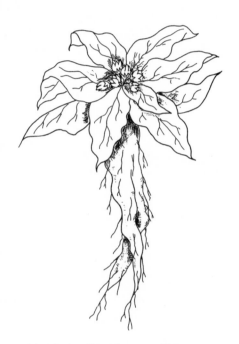

The flowers of the mandrake symbolize the enlightened soul that emerges from its material world experiences. The fruit of the mandrake represents the spiritual alchemy, the fruit that is produced through the completion of each incarnation. The leaves signify the influences that spread out into the world through the actions of the personality that is worn

Mandrake (*Mandragora officianarum* and *Mandragora autumnalis*)

by the soul. These are the keys to note in terms of laying out and crafting your magical intentions when using parts of the mandrake.

In the old lore of mandrake, there is a female spirit known as Mandragoritis—*She of the Mandrake*. This spirit oversees the plant itself and is called upon when working with mandrakes. Mandragoritis does not abide within the mandrake but instead controls the spirits that do (and in this regard can be thought of as their queen).

In mandrake lore the plants possess a gender nature. The "white mandrake" (*Mandragora officinarum*) is the male, and the "black mandrake" (*Mandragora autumnalis*) is the female plant. Some practitioners prefer to call the female spirit Mandragora and the male Mandragoro (in place of calling upon Mandragoritis). The simpler and, I believe, older way is to use the evocation "I call upon She of the Mandrake," and let it go at that. But it can also be useful to identify with the gender of each mandrake by using the male and female names.

Obtaining a live mandrake root can be very challenging. In some Witch Shops you may be able to find dried mandrake roots (sometimes mixed with leaves). In this case it is likely you will not know the gender of the plant. Also be aware that some companies sell the May Apple plant as a mandrake (probably because it has been called American mandrake). If you come by mandrake in this way, then it is best to evoke Mandragoritis (or Mandragora for a shortened form).

Blackthorn
(*Prunus spinosa*)

The spirit of the blackthorn is associated with the powers of the night and of shadow as well. Its spirit is called Sheadwa (pronounced Sheed-dwah) or he of the shadow. The advantage of using blackthorn is that you can summon magical energy that is pure. In other words, it comes directly from the realm of shadow, which has not been touched by human influences on the surface world. Therefore, it can be magically informed with the witch's intent and is void of anything inhibiting it or modifying it.

Blackthorn is keeper and revealer of secrets hidden beneath the earth within the shadow. Through it the witch can receive a vast store of magical knowledge. Traditionally, the witch uses a blackthorn wand or cane to wield the forces of shadow. In old lore a blackthorn cane is called a "blasting rod" and has the reputation for raising storms, damaging crops, and crushing enemies. In this light the blackthorn spirit is not one that adheres to the "harm none" philosophy found in many modern Wiccan systems.

The spirit of the hawthorn is associated with the powers of light and with the magical glimmer of the Faery Realm. Its spirit is called *Kwethanna* (pronounce qwee-thaw-na) or the *White Mistress*. Hawthorn is the opener of gateways or portals, and in this regard is the key-keeper of the doorway into the Faery Realm. Hawthorn aids the release of departed souls and directs them to the afterlife.

White Thorn
(*Crataegus monogyna*)

As a magical tool, the witch uses the hawthorn wand or cane for works of transformation and transition. These tools are also excellent for casting ritual circles and opening the portals to nonmaterial reality. The hawthorn also has a reputation as a guardian of thresholds, and in old lore it is coupled with the ash and oak tree. The combination of the three denotes the entryway to the Otherworld.

The spirit of rowan is associated with protection against enchantment. This is because it has power to summon allies from the mystical realms. The name of the spirit of rowan is *Reudwyn* (pronounced rude-win) or the *White Lady of the Red Blessing.*

Rowan (*Sorbus aucuparia*)

Rowanberries have the imprint of a dark five-pointed star where the stem attaches, and some people regard this as a reflection of its protective spirit. One magical use is to mark objects with the red juice of the berry by "painting" a pentagram.

The spirit of birch is intimately connected to souls of the dead. Her name is *Brydethe* (pronounced Bree-death) or *She Who Gathers the Dead.* In old lore, birch is used to direct wandering spirits of the dead.

Birch branches are used in some traditions as the sweep-end of a broom. As a tool the broom is used with the sweep in front or upright. This "herds" the dead or parts the way between them so that passage is allowed. Such lore is tied to the idea of the witch's broom in flight, upon which the witch traverses the Otherworld/Underworld.

The spirit of willow is associated with the Underworld and its entry at the center of the crossroads. The

Birch tree (*Betula alba*)

spirit is called *Weligwyn* (pronounced wah-lee-gwen) or *Lady of the White Tresses*. Willow is associated with oath-taking and the *binding* that is associated with initiation.

Willow tree
(*Salix babylonica*)

In old lore, strips of willow bark are used to bind thin birch branches to the ash handle of the witch's broom. This symbolizes the covenant between the witch and the night queen. In this regard, witches are the stewards of crossroads magic and gatekeepers at the entrance to the Otherworld.

The spirit of the walnut is associated with Otherworld guides, guardians, and allies. It is called *Wealhenin* (pronounced we-all-hey-nin) or *He Who Gifts*. In old lore the walnut is associated with Faeries and other beings that gift humans with needed items. In times of need, a gifted walnut is opened and from within it appears just what the person in the tales requires in order to accomplish a goal.

The walnut tree has deep roots into the realms below, and its power is drawn up by circular

Walnut tree (*Juglans regia*)

dances performed around its trunk. Its power is both fertile and sterilizing depending upon the way shadow is called through the tree.

The spirit of henbane is associated with barriers and fixing things in place. Its spirit is named *Necterra* (pronounced Nek-tear-rah) or *She Who Binds*. Henbane is used in spells and works of magic intended to block, bind, or stop activity.

Henbane
(*Hyoscyamus niger*)

Henbane is also useful in stopping communication. This concept may be related to the poisonous effect of its seeds on birds, who are often regarded as messengers. In any case, henbane can serve to disrupt or sever unwanted correspondence or contact. It is also useful against stopping gossip and lies.

The spirit of hemlock is associated with reparation. Its spirit is known as *Atonen* (pronounced A-tone-en) or *He Who Sets Right*. Hemlock is used in spells that serve to correct a situation or bring settlement in some lasting way.

Hemlock can also be used to help lovers reconcile through its ability to end strife and restore the previous relationship. Bear in mind that it is not the physical properties of the plant, it is the spirit that works through its connection.

The spirit of hellebore is associated with maintaining harmony. Its spirit is called *Ellebrina* (pronounced El-lah-bree-nah) or *She Who Calms*. Hellebore possesses the ability to appease disturbed spirits and is used in magic to deal with haunted sites. Such practices connected hellebore to exorcism.

Hemlock
(*Conium maculatum*)

The hellebore plant is also known as the Christmas rose, a curious name for this ancient plant. Various reasons are given for connecting the plant to the Christmas holiday, but the simplest explanation lies in its nature to create harmony. This feeling is often attached to the holiday season itself. But perhaps a more appropriate name is the Yule rose (if we are to give hellebore another name).

Hellebore
(*Helleborus niger*)

The spirit of nightshade is associated with invisibility (in the sense of going unnoticed). Its spirit is called *Atropa* (pronounced A-tro-pah) or *She of the Hidden Night* (some also call her the Faery-witch). Belladonna is often used in potions intended to vanquish enemies by gaining secret information about them.

Belladonna is used to enter the deeper levels of trance and dream states. In this light it is intimately connected with astral doorways, and thereby allows the "traveler-in-spirit" to be privileged to matters guarded on the material plane.

Nightshade
(*Atropa belladonna*)

The spirit of foxglove is associated with summoning. Its spirit is named *Tylanna* (pronounced Tie-lan-nah) or *She Who Calls the Fey*. Foxglove aids with communication with the Otherworld and helps gain rapport with the Faery.

Foxglove can be used in matters of love to call to a mate or to restore passion. It is considered to be most effective when used in spells that are cast on May Eve or Summer Eve. Both of the seasons are associated with the Faery, which brings us back full circle regarding the nature of foxglove.

Foxglove
(*Digitalis purpurea*)

The spirit of aconite is associated with the force of shadow and how it moves between the worlds. Its spirit is known as *Maestra* (pronounced may-ess-trah) or *Mistress of the Shadow*. Aconite is used to consecrate ritual and magic tools that work with shadow, and which are also used in the service of the Lady of the Crossroads.

In power, the aconite plant is second only to the mandrake. Both are connected to humans, which is meant to indicate that through them the human and plant worlds merge. Aconite is often called monkshood, denoting a humanoid connection, and the word "mandrake" has an obvious connection in both name and the shape its roots can take.

Aconite
(*Aconitum napellus*)

The spirit of wolfs-bane is associated with banishment. Its name is *Gebanshen* (pronounced Gebh-ann-shin) or *He Who Sends Away*. In this light wolfsbane is a banisher of undesired visitors, which includes spirits, animals, and humans. Wolfsbane is a good protector of the witch's garden.

Wolfsbane
(*Aconitum vulparia* or *lycoctonum*)

The lore of wolfsbane is tied to the idea of "elf shot" or "elf darts" in old lore. In such tales we find accounts of sharp objects dipped in its aconite juice that were used to scratch a person (the attacker going unnoticed in a crowd). The juice of the plant entered the bloodstream and brought about death. From this activity arose the idea that the "little people" shot arrows or threw darts to cause harm.

Where the Hallow Stands

Earlier in this book we touched on the idea that the spiritual-mindedness of the witch comes from primal concepts of the Old World. When we speak of the Old World, we are talking about a time when the seemingly mystical forces of nature were as real to our ancestors as was the everyday world. Lightning, thunder, earthquakes, and other phenomena evoked the presence of Otherworld forces.

It is in the ancient experience of old forests that various beliefs about the enchanted world of witches arose. All of the old European cultures populated the woods with a variety of spirits and beings. Often these creatures were regarded as dangerous to encounter, but in such stories the role of the human and his or her contribution to the problem is often missing from the tales. Rarely do these stories point out that the human is an intruder into the forest, and one who disrespects the world of its inhabitants.

It is noteworthy that in the old tales the witch often lives in the forest. She or he dwells outside of the villages or towns. This theme is a remembrance of the witch's connection to the untamed world. It also points to the witch as one who maintains a functional relationship with the spirits who inhabit the forest. In essence, these tales depict the witch as human and yet a full participant in the mystical or so-called supernatural world.

When we remove the political elements from the old tales, the Old World appears. It is a realm not ruled by humankind or contaminated by subjugation, greed, or the desire for excess wealth. Instead, it is subject to nature's rule, which means a balance in which everything is of equal importance to the whole. Everything contributes its full measure and everything receives back in accord.

In Old World witchcraft we find the belief in material reality and nonmaterial reality. These are the two equal halves of the greater reality they comprise. To simplify them, we call "material reality" the world of mortal-kind, and we refer to "nonmaterial reality" as the Spirit World, or Otherworld. Concerning material reality, we call its active forces "physics," and for nonmaterial reality the operative forces are known as "metaphysics." These principles are the body and soul of something greater than themselves.

We can now turn our attention to another principle, or mystical concept, which is known as the Hallow. Where material reality and nonmaterial reality meet is where the Hallow stands. It creates equilibrium and is an interfacing point through which both worlds can interplay. The witch can tap into this *poise*, and from it draw out some of its essence, which itself is the full potential of magic. Magic is the force of limitless possibility; it is the shared consciousness of material and nonmaterial reality. We touched on this concept in chapter three, where we looked at the merged consciousness of the guardian and the way-shower. As noted, they exchange part of their nature with each other. Through this exchange the conscious mind accepts something it has not experienced as though it did, and the subconscious mind regards an "imaged thing" as a material condition.

It is in the Hallow that things converge and where no argument or conflict exists. A convergence is when differences come together to achieve a common conclusion, result, or union. This is, at its core, the function of the Hallow; its purpose is to maintain equilibrium and to create a corridor. This passageway allows us to move back and forth between the worlds. In this regard, the witches' ritual circle is a type of hallow.

The mythos of the Hallow depicts it as standing in the center of the ancient primordial forest. This forest exists inside the earth, and it provides the inner life of the planet. Just as trees in the material realm produce carbon dioxide within the earth's atmosphere, the primordial forest generates the vapor for the force known as Shadow. All of this is an evolved concept for mystical and magical application, and is not intended to indicate a belief that the earth literally contains material worlds within it. It does, however, contain the memories of ancient civilizations that are now buried beneath it. Likewise, it also remembers all living beings absorbed into its soil. This is sometimes called the memory of the bone. We will visit this later as a magical concept.

The magical concept of Shadow conveys the idea that consciousness exists within the land. From a modern perspective we might say that the energy of all mental activity is absorbed into the soil and retained within the mineral formation of the earth. This is not unlike the New Age belief that crystals empower the mind, body, and spirits of humans. The deeper thought is that minerals also hold and maintain the integrity of the energy passed to them. From an occult perspective we can regard this as holding memory.

Intimately connected to the themes discussed in this section are the physical roots of plants. In a mystical sense the roots are envisioned as drawing Shadow up into the plants. We know that the roots of plants have fine hairlike threads that extract minerals from the soil. From an occult perspective minerals are the bones of the earth. Therefore, the fine threads absorb bone memory and make it available to the witch through the plant.

The larger part of the roots extracts water from the soil, and in an occult sense this is the blood of the land below the surface. Bone and blood are reunited through the plant, which becomes the new flesh. The spirit possesses the body and animates it in the sense of imbuing it with consciousness. It is through this inner mechanism that shadow is bridged.

If we use mandrake as an example, significant teachings can be conveyed. The genius of the plant contains the memory of its species. It knows everything about being a mandrake through its inherited memory of the collective consciousness of every mandrake that has ever lived. We can extend this idea to include another related concept. Every witch (or magic-user) whose body was absorbed into the earth had her or his knowledge pass into shadow. Therefore, this memory is available through the genius of the mandrake. It is through the roots that such knowledge is drawn from shadow. This requires not only the willingness of the mandrake to make it available; it also entails the witch's ability to establish rapport with the plant. This also requires the cooperation of the spirit inhabiting the plant. The witch, as a pharmaceute, has the needed edge.

In the plant world, trees possess the deepest roots, but they do not readily share shadow as willingly as do such plants as herbs. In part this is because the roots of a tree are guardians as opposed to transmitters. A misunderstanding of this magical principle appears in legends wherein trees protect against witchcraft. In common folktales, trees such as a rowan are believed to possess the power to keep away witches. This is but one example of how esoteric knowledge can be desecrated by exoteric lore.

One of the sacred trees of witchcraft is the walnut. A legendary one reportedly grew in or near the city of Benevento, Italy. In esoteric tradition the roots of the tree connected it with the Underworld. The ancestral spirits joined the living witches who encircled the tree at specific times of gathering. In Italian lore the walnut is intimately connected to the Faery Realm. In popular tales whenever a main character is in need of something in particular, he or she is given a walnut. When the nut is opened, from inside appears the needed object.

Mystical trees appear in many tales of magic and magical realms. There is always something that distinguishes them from worldly trees. In the case of the walnut tree at Benevento, it is the shade, which is said to be as black as night. Other mystical trees are found only in the Otherworld, or Faery, realm. Typically, these trees have a glimmer or shining light around them. In many of the tales these trees are white in color.

In Faery lore, particularly among the Celts, the color white indicates a Faery nature. One example is the mention that Faeries ride white horses. Use of the suffix "wyn" or "wen" (meaning white), in names connected to the Otherworld, as in the name of the goddess Cerridwen, is another example. White is also traditionally the color of death, which signifies the bone (that which remains after the flesh is gone).

One important element of tree lore associated with the Faery Realm is that of the tree hollow as a doorway. In many folktales the hollow spaces found in some trunks are depicted as portals through which mortals can enter the Faery World. Spirits may pass through them into the material world as well. In old tales a floating white light often leads mortals to trees that serve as doorways.

The legend of a white tree, or a tree of light, is an ancient theme. In some of the older lore we find the white birch tree connected with such tales, and it has long been associated with spirits of the dead. White trees are most often linked to the Faery Realm and serve as mystical beings. The tales created around magical trees, and the realms they occupy, encapsulate metaphors and mystical concepts in story form.

Many esoteric systems contain an inner mystery tradition that connects their structure to mystical concepts. In essence, such systems use imagery, lore, and stories to capture and convey these concepts. The settings, characters, themes, and events all represent mystical elements and their interaction. Through them, the teachings are conveyed in a conceptual way that includes embracing the parts as elements of the mystery concepts.

In the system of witchcraft known as Ash, Birch, and Willow, a mythos is in place that preserves elements of the old mystical teachings described in this chapter. It is a common element within mystery traditions to possess a mythos related to the view of nonmaterial reality. In ABW the concept exists of two key realms, or access realms, rooted in the mystery tradition mythos. These realms are known as *LuNeya* (pronounced Loo-Nay-ah) and *Faewyn* (Pronounced Fay-win). The first is conceived of as a *Moon world* where souls abide while awaiting reincarnation. In the mythos it is an island with a city called Morphos. A dense forest known as the Woods of Proserpina surrounds the city, and the island is covered with poppies and mandrakes. In the center of the island is a high hill with an opening leading down into the Cavern of Hecate.

The White Tree

In the ABW mythos the realm of the dead is connected to the earth through the sacred White Tree of LuNeya. Departed souls of the dead journey along its branches, which is a metaphor for the process of reincarnation. In the mythos they are accompanied by beings known as the Seven Sisters, who usher the dead through the gateways. These are associated with the Pleiades and are most notably marked on the eves of May and November.

In the Faery Realm, called the land of Faewyn, is the sister tree known as the White Tree of Faewyn. Although the trees are two, we can regard them as one tree seen from different sides. The Land of Faewyn can be thought of as the spiritual counterpart of earth. It has geography but is comprised of light instead of matter. This light is so condensed that it takes on tangible form. It is, however, always in a high state of vibration and reacts to thoughts. Just as on earth we can shape the landscape with tools and equipment, the Faery people can shape it with their minds.

The Faery are more advanced than humans, and their technology produces results that can cause humans to believe that things are accomplished through magic. Their technology also allows them to pass through into other dimensions. Long ago they explored the material plane and came into contact with humans. The limited understanding of our ancestors concerning the Faery Race left us with the myths and legends we now possess.

Just as the White Tree of LuNeya allows souls to journey, the White Tree of Faewyn serves as a network of passageways into other dimensions. The Faery no longer directly enter the material realm as they once did, but contact is still made between the worlds. The White Tree is one of the symbols of communication with the Faery Race and also appears as a symbol of alliance with them.

The White Tree of LuNeya is pictured with seven stars above its branches. These are the Pleiades, also known as the Seven Sisters. In old lore the Pleiades mark the gates between the world of the living and the world of the dead. The Pleiades align with the horizon on earth at the May festival and the October festival. Here we see them as positioned opposite at each season. May is associated with life and October with death—the Gates of Life and Death.

Whenever the White Tree is associated with the Faery Realm, it appears in symbolism without the seven stars. We can think of it as an aspect of the one tree that serves as a gateway into the Faery Realm. In ancient lore the Faeries and spirits of the dead were believed to be the same thing. According to this lore, the ancient burial mounds later became viewed as Faery hills, and the legend of an inner world developed around the myths and legends. An ancient Etruscan belief held that souls of the dead could become Faeries in the other realm. This is tied to another Etruscan belief that souls can eventually become gods or demi-gods. In some systems it is believed that souls gain power as they reincarnate, and through this they can become powerful entities in the Otherworld.

Old Ones of the Forest

Earlier we touched on the idea that the spiritual-mindedness of the witch arose from the experience of the ancient forest. For Old World witches the modern idea of a "God of Witchcraft" is rooted in the concept of *He of the Shadowy Wooded Places*. The idea of a "Goddess of Witchcraft" is tied to the concept of *She of the White Round*. These are the Old Ones, a term given them long before the idea of Goddess and God as we know it today.

While I am not at liberty to provide the name for the God-figure, he is the presence of the forest itself. The "mind" of the forest is his awareness. He is not the forest per se, for the forest is a mechanism of life and death. He is the usher. The Goddess is the presence of light in the shadowy places of the deep forest. The two are united in the imagery of tree branches against a full moon at night. This is the Old Ones embracing. From this union their children are born in the blackness of space and also within the depths of the forest where shade is blackness.

In the Old Ways lore when He of the Forest wishes to appear to humans, he takes on the shape of a stag with a full set of antlers. The antlers symbolize the tree branches. When She of the White

Round makes her presence known to humans, she shines as the full moon through the tree branches of the forest.

An old tradition exists that is formed around two tree branches. Both are of the stang variety, which means a branch that terminates in a "Y" formation. The one representing He of the Forest is left untrimmed so that the forks have the look of stag antlers. The stang representing She of the White Round is trimmed smooth without any twigs or offshoots on it. They are used in a variety of ways that are explained later on.

The forest is also home to other beings that are among the Old Ones. They are primordial spirits that attach themselves to the trees. When a particularly powerful spirit has been connected to a specific tree for a very long time, the tree takes on a different look from those around it. To humans the tree appears to have a face of some sort. Such faces appear in Medieval art and contemporary fantasy art as well. It is important to take note of such trees and to ensure that no damage is done them. No good can come from desecrating the tree or forcing such an ancient being out of the tree by felling it.

One of the tales associated with trees features what is often referred to as the leaf-people. In this lore it is said that the leaves of trees are the bodies of the leaf-people. These spirits are messengers of the forest. They speak to each other through the wind that blows through the trees. The will of the forest is made known through the whispering of the leaf-people, and they are intimately connected to He of the Forest in many ways, for, as noted earlier, he is associated with the mind of the forest. The next time you hear the rustling of the leaves, something "Otherworld" may draw your ear.

Another associated tale states that the leaf-people withdraw into the trees in the season of fall. As the spirits abandon the leaves, they fall to the ground. In essence these are the bones lying on the forest floor. In the spring the leaf-people are reborn through the branches as new leaves appear.

The race of beings we call the Faery also belong to the classification of Old Ones. In Old World witchcraft they are regarded as Otherworld beings that are native to their realm. Other traditions view Faeries as fallen angels or beings from another planet, but Old Ways witches do not share these ideas. Instead, the Faery Race is held to be a very ancient race in a parallel world beyond the veil that separates material reality from nonmaterial reality.

There are many legends that provide accounts of meetings between humans and Faeries. The earlier ones are usually positive experiences, but over time we find a decline in the goodwill of the Faeries. Among the pleasant tales we find the lore of the Silver Bough. It is described as a branch from an apple tree, silver in color and bearing a number of apples. The Silver Bough is given to mortals by the Faery Queen as an invitation to enter the Faery Realm. It provides safe passage, and the apples serve as food for the traveler. The legends go on to describe the apples, which make a sound like tiny bells when touched or shaken. The sound of the apples causes humans to forget their cares.

The tale of the Silver Bough is but one of many that include enchanted trees. In general these trees, or some part of them, grant access to hidden realms. One classic example is the *Faery door* in the hollow of a trunk. These are metaphors for altered states of consciousness that open awareness of the hidden realms. Once realized, these portals can be used to interface with mystical realms. The plant kingdom is one such dimension.

Interfacing with the Plant

In Old World witchcraft, there are methods of intimately connecting the witch to the plant realm. In modern practice an altar is used. It is set with the mortar in the center of the altar. The pestle is placed upright inside the mortar so that it stands like a pillar. Depending upon the shape of your set, some material may be needed inside the mortar to nest the pestle so that it remains upright. Decorations of the season are placed around the mortar as well as inside. Once decorated, the mortar and pestle become the focal point of the altar, which creates the matrix through which you can interface with the plant realm.

The arrangement of the mortar and pestle represents the active and fertile relationship between the feminine and masculine. The pestle is upright and inside the mortar that symbolizes the womb of nature. The seasonal plants create the alignment to the tide of nature. To enter into the sacred space of this imagery, simply focus your attention on the mortar and pestle and speak the words of joining:

> Seed to sprout, sprout to leaf,
> Leaf to bud, bud to flower,
> flower to fruit, fruit to seed.
> Shadow to spirit, spirit to earth,
> Earth to season, season to plants,
> Plants to tender, tender to garden,
> Garden to magic, magic to mortar and pestle

Now cup the mortar between the palms of your hands. Close your eyes and envision a tree with roots extending down into the earth and branches reaching upward into the sky. Mentally move

CDortar & Pestle

this image into your body so that you become the trunk of this tree. Once you have this firmly in your mind's eye, then *feel* the roots extending downward from the lower half of your body. Next, *feel* the branches raising up from your upper half. You are now connected.

A connection with nature in this particular stream of energy aids the witch in maintaining inner rapport with the Green World. The rapport, in turn, ensures that the plant spirits will work with you as needed. Use the alignment through the mortar and pestle as a spiritual practice. This will link you with the forces of the *white round*, which influence the cycle of plant life. This refers to the cycle of the moon, and to its culmination in the full moon.

Prayers, requests, and blessings can be directed through the mortar and pestle. They can be directed down into the earth to connect with ancestors or departed souls. This is done by envisioning the roots of the tree as you speak. Likewise, your intentions can be directed into the celestial realms through the imagery of the branches.

The best results are obtained by establishing a routine. You can perform your alignments and connect to lunar forces at the new moon, half moon, and full moon. This will recharge you. During the waning moon you can use the alignment to release negative energy as a means of purification. Direct the energy into the soil but not down into the depths of shadow.

Working with the Mortar and Pestle

When we think of the witch as one of the plant people, there is no tool more pertinent to the witches' craft than the mortar and pestle. Through this tool the witch literally gathers, prepares, refines, and blends the substance of magic. There is no greater hands-on approach to magic than that of the mortar and pestle set.

In the Book of Magic section you will find complete instructions for using the mortar and pestle, but for now there are a few things to note in advance. The mortar and pestle are the primary tools of the magical art. The set is used to connect the witch with the Hallow, which places her or him in the center of magic itself. A variety of spells can be performed with the mortar and pestle. The set represents the ability of the witch to stir magical forces, integrate them, and pour them out into the world. Through this mental alignment, empowerment lies in the hands of the witch.

The mortar represents the womb of nature, but also the shadow force beneath the earth. Through these connections the mortar collects, pools, and regenerates. In this sense it is the birthing womb of magic. The mortar is also the tomb that receives the dead; therefore, the mortar bears the title *of Life-giver* and *Death-taker*.

The pestle symbolizes the phallus through which the seeds of life are directed. It is also the ancient sacred standing-stone and the herms figure at the crossroads (described later). Through these connections the pestle fertilizes and initiates the forces of manifestation. It directs the magical forces that are drawn to the mortar, and there it sanctifies the substances placed within the mortar. Just as the pestle can direct vitality, it can also create a flaccid state of being. Therefore, the pestle is known as the *Horn-awakener* and the *Serpent-slumberer*.

The material from which the mortar and pestle is made will bring a specific alignment into play. I prefer one made of wood when working with plants, and one made of stone when working with shadow. In effect, wood is a practical link to plants, and stone (being mineral) connects to what lies beneath the surface of the earth (in this case, Shadow). You can experiment with different materials or use one that currently has meaning for you. In a mundane practical sense, note that a wooden mortar will absorb chemicals from plants and needs to be thoroughly cleansed. Cleansing is more effective for polished stone or metal mortars. There are other factors you will want to take into account when selecting the material for your mortar and pestle. These include the weight of the set and the wear and tear likely to occur when operating the mortar and pestle.

When using the mortar and pestle, you will be working in motion and sound. Motion involves moving the pestle in either a clockwise or counterclockwise circling within the mortar. Sound involves tapping the pestle rhythmically against the inside of the mortar. These things connect with occult principles related to the inner mechanism of magic.

A clockwise movement builds energy, which is reflected in nature where we see that high pressure systems move in a clockwise pattern. This type of system gathers clouds and produces rain. By contrast, low pressure systems move counterclockwise and thereby break up weather patterns and disperse cloud formations.

Tapping the pestle is connected to trance inducement and to the magical principle of the ritual knell or toll. When speaking an enchantment, you tap the pestle in a measured meter to accompany the words. In most cases the meter is a simple count of 1-2-3-4 (pause), 1-2-3-4, and so on. You will develop your own sense of metering as you gain proficiency in the art.

The mortar and pestle are held in one of two ways. When the mortar contains material substances, it is always held upright. After the contents are poured out, then the mortar is held sideways. In this position the pestle is inserted into the mortar. It is then spun around in a wheel-like motion (similar to the way the crank on a fishing rod is turned). In spell casting, a forward circular motion is used for gain and a reverse movement serves to dissolve and weaken. Blessing and quelling work operate through this method as well. To quell is to put a stop to behavior intended to cause distress, suffering, affliction, or annoyance. This is sometimes referred to as un-vexing.

Working with Plants

As mortal beings, we share a relationship with the plants that are also dependent upon the earth itself. The lineage of the witch as a pharamceute reveals the bonding between plant and witch. The inner spirit of the witch and that of the plant remember the power of each other for their memories reside in the essence of shadow beneath the earth.

The witch and the plant share a mortal condition wherein the living spirit is encased in a material form, which is bound to the earth. The spirits of both plant and witch are also connected to celestial forces and the seasonal cycles of nature (as well as the tides of inner and outer space). It is through this connection that the witch becomes a seer. In this way plants serve as pathways of vision through which the witch can peer down into the memory of the earth or up into the starry skies where branches point the way. Through the trunk or stem, the witch has access to the Faery gate between the worlds. It is here in the middle realm that we can look outward through the Faery door, and see the astral images that foretell what is likely to manifest in the material world if nothing alters the forming patterns. This is, at its core, the mechanism of divination.[67]

For the Old Ways witch the cycles of power are those associated with the agricultural seasonal shifts. The Spring Equinox marks the tide of renewal, and the Autumn Equinox marks the tide of decline. These, respectively, are the forces of summoning and releasing. The first shoots to appear in the spring can be harvested and made into an incense or oil for summoning. The first leaves to wither or drop can be made into an incense or oil for releasing connections.

The Summer Solstice marks the tide of growth, and the Winter Solstice marks the tide of preservation. The first fruits or vegetable of the summer season can be harvested and made into potions to attract abundance. The last remaining leaves of winter, being the evergreen, can be harvested and made into sachets to aid in preserving and persevering. In effect, the witch captures the essence of the power that is most concentrated in any given season. This is the way of the pharmaceute.

The time of the year that falls directly between each solstice and equinox is known as the cross quarter. Traditionally, these mark ancient celebrations that fall on the Eve of a festival. Because they take place at night, they are associated with shadow. Portions of the earth's shadow force emerge at night and surround a plant. This is the most efficacious time to harvest magical plants.

The act of harvesting a plant is surrounded with ceremony and protocol. Traditionally, the harvesting tool should be made of sharpened bronze or copper. These metals do not disrupt the energy of the indwelling spirit of the plant. Metals such as iron or steel can disturb the energy of a plant spirit and needlessly taint the extracted shadow in an unfavorable way. This is tied to the lore that the Faery Race abhors iron. From a metaphysical perspective, iron and steel interact with magnetism, whereas bronze and copper do not. Magnetic fields can interfere with the natural ways of plant spirits and Faeries.

When harvesting a plant, you will take only portions of it and rarely all of it. The plant must be approached with reverence, and it needs to be informed of the harvesting moment. This is traditionally accomplished through the "song of the harvester," which can be hummed, whistled, or played on an instrument such as a flute. You can choose your own tune for this purpose. Begin you harvester song as you approach the plant from a distance of several feet.

When you are near the plant, walk around it three times and sprinkle purified water in a circle that encloses it. Speak to the plant and explain that you require its assistance. Next you will need to offer it something in exchange for the part of the plant you are taking. Choose something that is nontoxic to plants so that the soil is not contaminated. In the grimoire section of this book, you will find some desirable choices.

Once the part of the plant is harvested, make sure that it does not touch the earth. If it does, part or all of its shadow may withdraw back into the soil. Traditionally, the harvested material is immediately wrapped in a silk handkerchief. Ideally, until the material is used, it should be placed in a closed box throughout the day so that the sunlight does not fall upon it.

As noted earlier, when working with plants from an occult perspective, each has a body and a spirit. Within the plant there is also the blood and the ether, which correspond to the means through which the plant is enlivened. When the blood of the plant is gone along with its spiritual counterpart (ether), the bones remain behind. These are the dry stems and leaves. From them a ground powder can be made, which is referred to as dust. The substance is made for specific purposes from particular types of plants. The plants are selected from a table of correspondences that guides the practitioner in her or his choices.

The magical dust of plants is used in various ways for several purposes. Remember that dust is the powdered bone and that bone contains memory. This memory includes the land and the shadow beneath. One example is "graveyard dust" made from the root or bark of a tree growing in a cemetery. A misunderstanding of this magical principle resulted in the use of soil from a grave (dust being misconstrued for soil). Such soil draws only upon the precise grave zone itself and not the spirit of the cemetery as a whole. A tree, through its roots, takes in the spirit of the land, and if that land is a cemetery, then it draws in its spirit collectively. So to make and possess "graveyard dust" is to capture the shadow of the dead. This substance is powerful when used for divination, spirit contact, or to work with chthonic forces in general.

Traditionally, to launch the magical intent of dust, it is sprinkled across thresholds, across walkways, or in some place where it will come into contact with a person. An envelope or letter can be dusted, or it can be sent upon the breath or through the wind. The presence of dust instills the memory of its shadow and the intent of the witch who creates it. In effect, dust attaches magical intent to a place or person. In chapter five you will be introduced to the tool know as the ritual platter. When using this tool, magical dust can be added to the ashes to amplify or expand magical intention (see Grimoire).

Dust can be transformed and reconnected with the living genii by restoring moisture. The benefit is that this draws the intelligence of the plant kingdom back into contact with the material. Through this the living spirit of the plant can be present "out of season" when the physical plant would naturally be absent above ground. An easy method of accomplishing this is to add three drops of liquid chlorophyll in a mortar, add a pinch of the plant material, and use the pestle to mix them together. This is, in effect, a reanimation of the bones.

The Shadow Garden

One of the most powerful witch gardens is that of growing shadow. The idea is to have a section of the garden dedicated to adding libations and nontoxic debris from each ritual. In most cases this will be ash from the burning of incense, wine, and fragments of the ritual feast. The ash is scattered around the garden and the wine is poured onto the soil. Food is buried in the ground. Because these things have been imbued with ritual energy, they can pass power into the garden. This establishes the presence of your magic in the garden itself.

The idea can be expanded into a Wheel of the Year garden. For this purpose, you make a circular garden border and mark it into eight distinct divisions. Each one represents one of the eight Sabbats. Establish plants at each of the eight points, and these plants are chosen for their association with the season. When selecting each plant, think in terms of incorporating them into a Sabbat ritual. In other words, what parts of the plants can enhance the rites?

Once the garden is established, you can add ritual fragments to the section associated with the specific Sabbat. In other words, after a Winter Solstice ritual you can work the remnants into the soil of the section assigned to this season. Each season and section of the garden is united in this way. In performing this operation, you will be charging the plants with the energy connected to the seasonal rite. This will develop an impressive force within your seasonal plants.

After the first complete cycle of the year, you can then begin to harvest parts of the plants for each Sabbat as it arrives. The plants can be used in whatever way works for your sense of ritual.

You may choose to place some leaves or the root of a nontoxic/non-poisonous plant into the chalice of wine, or you may want to add some parts to the incense as it burns. Flowers, buds, or fruit can be set on the altar. The idea is simply to enhance the ritual by using plants charged from past Sabbats.

The occult teachings behind this method relate to the force of shadow beneath the soil. When you place ritual fragments in the garden, they are absorbed into the immediate area of the garden. The plants take in some of the magical energy, and the fragments are eventually broken down into elements by the soil. This act passes the energy into shadow memory. The plant draws this refined energy back into its being, and the power of the plant is increased twofold.

In addition to incorporating the seasonal plants into a ritual or spell, you can also place dried leaves or part of a root into a small pouch. This can be carried on the person so as to imbue one with the magical energy. Carrying a magical charge in this way works its way into the aura surrounding the flesh body. The aura then reflects the essence of the magic passed to it. One practical use is to carry a pouch of leaves or a root from the November Eve celebration, which is associated with spirits of the dead. You can have the pouch with you when performing divination or seeking communication with the dead.

It is noteworthy that several of the magical plants and trees of witchcraft are related to the rose. Examples of the latter are the hawthorn, blackthorn, rowan, apple, and willow. For the purposes of this chapter, the rose plant can serve as a "go-between" spirit to put you into contact with spirits from related plants. This also means that the spirit of the rose can tap into the shadow associated with related powers and memories. If you cannot obtain a tree such as a hawthorn or blackthorn, then working with the spirit of the rose is a functional alternative.

Roses feature prominently in many occult paths and symbolism. Participants in the ancient rites of Dionysus wore garlands of roses to protect themselves from revealing secrets while intoxicated with wine. In this light the rose is a symbol of oath bound knowledge that is not to be revealed to noninitiates. In some contemporary witchcraft traditions, the rose still symbolizes this practice. In occult tradition we find the term "*sub rosa,*" which translates as "under the rose" and denotes the rule of secrecy. From this idea comes the practice of setting a rose in the presence of any assembly where secrets are being discussed.

The Power of the Rose

In Old World witchcraft two roses are present whenever someone is admitted into training in the witch arts. A red rose represents dedication to the ways, and it is the sign of she or he who will aid the continuance of the witches' craft. A white rose symbolizes the bone (and therefore the memory) of all who lived the ways since the time of the beginning. In seasons where

roses are not available, their images are present during initiatory rites.

A modern practice is to connect with the spirit of the rose lineage through a simple rite performed before a rosebush (any color
is fine, but red is preferred). To begin, you will need to have with
you, four roses with stems and thorns (two white and two red). A
single red and white rose are placed next to each other, and the
others are kept next to you for later use.

The two roses you are working with are set as follows. The one
on the left is the white rose and on the right is the red one. A
thorn is taken from each rose. The white thorn is used to prick the
left index finger and the red thorn pricks the right index finger. A
drop of blood is touched, respectively, to each rose. The roses are
then buried together in front of the rosebush while you face west.

Over the rose grave the words of joining are spoken:

> I summon now the spirit of the Rose,
> remember only what the ancestor knows,
> my blood calls through your fragrant breath,
> grant now the sacred union I request.

Immediately after speaking these words, pick up the roses
beside you and inhale the fragrance of each rose, first the white
and then the red. As you take in the scent, you are receiving
the blessings of the rose spirit. Repeat the inhalation three
times.

You are now ready to call upon the spirit of the rose for the
purpose of connecting you to it and its relatives. Present the white
and red rose to the rosebush. Then create a circle around the bush
using the petals from these roses. Alternate white and red petals

as you lay the circle out in a clockwise fashion. Once the circle is prepared, place the palms of both hands, separated, inside the circle at its base.

Look directly at the rosebush for a few moments, and then speak these words:

I call upon She of Thorn-blooded Rose.

Now draw your eyes down to the base of the bush and focus on where it meets the ground. Then speak these words, exhaling after the first line and deeply inhaling following the second:

I send forth the breath of life into your roots,
And draw up the shadow memory.

This joins you to the spirit of the rose and through her to the lineage connecting within the shadow embraced by her roots. To call upon these spirits, use the plant spirit seals in the Book of Calls (see the grimoire section of this book).

The Witch's Staff

In Old World witchcraft we find the use of the sacred branch. This is the witch's staff, which is taken from a particular tree. The type of tree is chosen by the witch due to a special connection she or he feels toward it. In some circles the chosen tree is referred to as the Patroness or Patron of the witch. Among the most popular are the ash, oak, willow, and apple. All of these have mystical and magical connections in old witch lore. To carry a staff is to walk with the power of the tree spirit.

Two other branches are used as tools in the art of witchcraft, and fall under the category of the *stang*. Earlier in the chapter we noted their connection to He of the Forest and She of the White Round. Her branch is used to outline the ritual circle on the ground for she is the "round" itself. Her globe of light in the night sky is symbolized by marking it on the earth as a circle. The stang representing the masculine connection is used to open and close the entrance to the ritual circle and to open the portals to the Otherworld. As previously noted, He of the Shadowy Wooded Places is connected to the cycle of life and death. Therefore, he is, in effect, a gatekeeper, and the stang represents his presence at the rites.

To create a ritual circle, you must first etch it into the ground by dragging the end of the feminine stang around the site. This process begins in the east and completes there again. When any person needs to leave or enter the marked circle, the masculine stang is used to create an opening through the perimeter. This is accomplished by inserting the "antlers" at the top of the stang into the edge of the circle at the east quarter. The stang is lowered to the ground and then moved upward, followed by a right to left movement. To reseal the circle this movement is performed in reverse.

During the ritual, the masculine stang is set standing at the southern quarter of the circle. The feminine stang is placed standing at the northern quarter. Both symbolize the presence of the Old Ones of the forest. A symbol representing the moon is suspended from the feminine stang. This can be a white shell, a stone, or a disk. The masculine stang bears an antler tip hanging from a cord, and at the base of the stang is placed the figure of a human skull.

Whenever a ritual is performed outside of a forest setting, the presence of She of the White Round can be summoned with the masculine stang. To do so, simply raise the stang and view the moon through the "antlers" on the end of the branch. Then speak the words of summoning as given in the Book of Calls. Next close your eyes and lower the end of the stang to about waist level. Then open your eyes and place the stang to the right of the feminine stang so that they now stand together.

In this chapter we have explored the world of the witch as it connects with the plant realm and its spirits. It is time now to come to an understanding of the extended magical world of the witch. In the following you will find the Arts of Witchcraft divided into three special categories. Let us move now to the next chapter where we will open the Grimoire of the Witches' Craft.

Chapter Five

THE BOOKS OF WITCHCRAFT:
A WITCH'S GRIMOIRE

It is a popular theme today that witches never possessed handwritten books. When we consider that illiteracy was high in days of old, it is not unreasonable to take this position. But the tradition of a secret witch's book still persists. One argument is that illiterate witches used symbols instead of an alphabet, and were taught the meanings of these signs. By the use of these symbols, the witch could learn and perform the timeless works of witchcraft, or so it is said. But could such an old tradition of a witch's book have any basis in fact?

The ancient Roman poet Horace provides one of the oldest references to a witch's book. This appears in his work titled *The Epodes*, which contains a tale of the witch known as Canidia. Horace describes an encounter with a witch who possesses a book containing magical incantations. He tells us that by the use of this book, witches can call down the moon from the night sky. Historian Owen Davies comments that Horace depicts Canidia as a prostitute-witch. He goes on to say that "high-class prostitutes" of the period were known to be literate. Davies remarks that they could have possessed books containing spells. He concludes there is no reason to assume that literate women of the period were less likely to use grimoires than were men.[68]

Tracking references to books allegedly used by witches reveals some interesting lore. Scholar Montague Summers, in his book *History of Witchcraft and Demonology*, mentions a book used by witches that has different colored pages and inks. Summers describes a witches' book called the *Red Book of Appin*, and another is simply referred to as *Devil's Missal*. Its pages are described as black and crimson. Summers goes on to say that witches read from a book whose cover is soft and hairy like a wolf's skin. Some of the pages are white and red, and others are black.[69]

The Witch Hunter known as Francesco Guazzo, in his seventeenth-century work titled the *Compendium Maleficarum*, mentions in Book One (chapter six) that a black book is used by witches. It is brought out during the witches' assemblies, and their names are recorded on its pages. Guazzo goes on to describe an event in 1594 that involved a gathering of witches. He states that a young woman was taken to a field on the eve of the Summer Solstice. She was led to a circle traced on the ground with a beech twig. Shortly thereafter, a small group of witches gathered and one of them read from a black book (Book One, chapter twelve).

Author W.G. Waters, in his work titled *The Facetious Nights of Straparola* (1901), writes an interesting passage: "When the appointed hour for the meeting had come, the witch took her little book in hand and drew a circle on the ground; then, having surrounded the same with certain magic signs and figures, she poured out some subtle liquid from a flask and drank a drop of it and gave as much to Isabella."[70]

References to the witches' book continue into contemporary folkloric studies. Italian professor Donato Bosca writes about contemporary witches in Piedmont, Italy, who reportedly are descended from a lineage of witches. He refers to them as the *Masche*, an Italian word meaning "the masked ones" or "the masked people." Bosca began studying the Masche in 1979, and ended up interviewing some contemporary practitioners during his research. He reveals several interesting aspects reported in his interviews with them. Among them is the traditional usage of a book, which is called *Il Libro del Commando* (The Book of Command).[71]

The Masche informed Bosca that their knowledge is hereditary and is passed through the maternal line. They said that "the power" is passed from an elder to a younger descendant. They admit that their art includes spells and potions that can heal as well as harm. Their Book of Command is handwritten using different colored inks. The mention of different colored inks is something we saw noted in past references to a witches' book.

Whether or not such books ever existed, or if in the past, witches' produced their own books, is not something I wish to argue for or against. My intention is to simply share some interesting lore related to the subject. We know that many witches today produce what some call a *Book of Shadows*. Author Gerald Gardner in his writings that appeared in the mid 1960s popularized its usage. Whatever the facts are about a witches' book, it seems wise to preserve spells and rituals in this way.

In the following pages I present three "books" of witchcraft. They fall under the subtitles: *Ways*, *Calls*, and *Magic*. Each contains material pertinent to the theme. I like this arrangement because it feels old and was the way in which material was passed to me in my early training. Perhaps there is a touch of nostalgia at work here.

The material contained in this book does not represent an ancient cohesive tradition of witchcraft. In other words, I am not claiming that an ancient sect of witches existed that used the material in the form given in this chapter. What I offer instead is a collection of very old practices, themes, and concepts of Old World witchcraft. The fashion in which they are represented is my own, but it is in keeping with how such things have been applied in the art of witchcraft over the centuries. In this regard the material is ever ancient and ever new.

A Witch's Grimoire

The tools of Old World witchcraft are simple and common items. The primary working tool is the mortar and pestle. It is used in a variety of ways that include its symbolism and its function as a ritual and magical tool. Symbolically, the mortar is a feminine vessel and represents a magical womb. It is called the *Life-giver* and *Death-taker* when used in some of the rituals. The pestle is a masculine symbol and represents the phallus. It is called the *Horn-awakener* and the *Serpent-slumberer* when used for magical means.

The secondary tool is called the platter. It can be any plate that is specifically set aside for ritual and magical use, but a light-colored one is best. Traditionally, the plate is covered in a layer of soot from the hearth. Fingertips are used to draw the needed symbols into the soot, which appear in contrast with the exposed areas of the plate underneath. Another method is to use the ashes of herbs that are chosen for specific correspondences related to the ritual or spell work at hand. In each technique you are drawing symbols into the ash that appear as it is wiped away by your finger.

Other tools of Old World witchcraft include the knife, wand, cauldron, branch, skull figure, and Ghost Stone. The knife is used for cutting and carving in both the material and spirit world. The wand is used for working with forces and entities. For magical and ritual purposes, the cauldron and the skull are often used together as a means of connecting with the dead. The branch is used to trace out a ritual circle on the ground, and to mark it in ways that are covered later in this chapter. Our final tool is the Ghost Stone, which is used to temporarily wield needed influence over spirits of the dead.

One of the last items used in Old World witchcraft is not technically a tool, but it does serve as a vessel. It is a bowl or gourd used to contain soil and/or soot, and is called the Ash Pot. Other bowls can be used as needed for ritual ashes that contain power, and for various fluids that are incorporated into rituals and works of magic.

Beginning in Blackness

Everything is born or issues forth from the black procreative state. We were born from the blackness within the womb into the material world where light abides. The sun and the moon seemingly rise from the black space of the Underworld as they ascend into the world of mortal kind. Just as things come from blackness, so too do they return there in the repeating cycle of birth, life, death, and renewal.

The first step into the ways of Old World witchcraft is to awaken the witch within; we can also regard this as an alignment to the ancient current. The technique is known as "The Call," which involves connecting with Otherworld spirits or deities. The earliest references to witches calling upon a deity come from pre-Christian literature, and so the concept is extremely ancient.

On the first night of the dark moon (the period of three moonless nights) go to a crossroads. In Northern Europe a crossroads is typically where four roads meet. In Southern Europe it is where three roads intersect to form a Y shape. Either formation will work fine and is a matter of personal choice.

There are several items you will need to bring with you to the crossroads:

1. Mortar and pestle
2. Platter
3. Bowl
4. Knife
5. Wand
6. Crossroad candle
7. Food offering
8. A pouch to fill with soil
9. A lock of your hair or nail clippings

One of the traditional items is very rare today but can be substituted with relative ease. The old item is known as a crossroad candle, and is a dried mandrake leaf that has been rolled into the form of a candle (mature mandrake leaves are about six to nine inches long). In some folk magic systems this is called the Devil's candle. For a substitute, you can rub oil on a candle and then roll it in dried mandrake leaves or roots. The candle should be black and at least six inches long.

Find a crossroads of dirt paths, or take a sack of soil with you to pour out on a path that is paved. This will provide the soil needed for marking. Once you are at the crossroads go to its direct center and press the mouth of the mortar into the earth. Turn it three times to form a circle in the soil. Lift it away and then use a finger to draw the witch's mark inside the circle on the ground.

Witch's Mark

On the left side of the witch's mark (inside the circle) set the crossroad candle upright. Between you and the mark, place the food offering on the platter (outside of the circle). Using your wand, trace over the crossroads, moving left to right. When finished, kneel and hold the wand up to the night sky with your left hand. Then say the following words:

> *I call upon the Three Daughters of Night,*
> *to come to the crossroad's candlelight.*
> *[Light the candle]*
> *All do approach, and I pray thee hark*
> *To words spoken over the witch's mark.*

Pick up the mortar and place the lock of your hair inside it. Next, press the end of the pestle on the hair so that it is firmly held against the inside of the mortar. Then recite these words:

> *By bone and blood, the path well worn,*
> *from common to mystical now transform.*
> *I awaken within me, the one with sight,*
> *The witch who lives mysteries of black sacred night.*

Next, pour out the lock of hair on top of the witch's mark in the soil. Then, using your wand, draw a triangle around the witch's mark in the soil. One of the tips needs to be facing you. Once drawn, sit comfortably in place with your eyes closed for a few moments. One very old practice involved pricking the skin and allowing three drops of blood to drip on the witch's mark.

Sit in place holding the candle until it is almost burned out completely. In the remaining light, use the knife to "cut" around the triangle in the soil. Then shovel the soil bearing the triangle, witch's mark, and hair into the bowl. Afterwards, pour the soil into the pouch (where it will remain for later use). End this stage by saying:

> *To the Three Daughters of Night, I give thanks at this site,*
> *for coming as in old to this thrice ancient rite.*
> *By the powers above and the forces below,*
> *As it was in the past, now too is it so.*

Pick up the pouch of soil and touch it to your forehead, heart area, genitals, and left foot as you recite:

> *Head and toe, all in-between do I give,*
> *mind, spirit, and body for as long as I live.*

Finish up by collecting everything for removal except for the offering of food. This is to be buried near the crossroads. Take any remaining wax with you for later use. Return home with the items. Before going to sleep, place the bag of soil beneath your pillow and leave it there for three nights.

Blessing in Light

The first step on to the path of Old World witchcraft involved beginning in blackness. Now it is time to step into the light of the moon where there is enlightenment in the places of darkness. By the light of the full moon you will bless your tools of the witches' craft.

Needed items

1. Branch for tracing circle
2. Mixture of the herbs rue, Saint-John's-wort, and vervain
3. Your knife
4. Your wand
5. Your mortar and pestle
6. A platter
7. A broom
8. A stang

Preparation

On the night of the full moon, take your branch and trace a circle on the ground large enough to allow room for you to move about easily. Once you have traced your circle, look up at the moon and point to it with your right hand. At the same time, using your left hand, point to the circle on the ground. Then say these words:

> *Circle of light, above in full glow*
> *I join thee now to the circle below*

Immediately walk around the inside of the circle with your palms facing downward, and trace over the circle three times. Recite as you walk:

> Moon *above and moon below*
> *mirror shining mystic glow*

Next, walk around the circle and sprinkle the herbal mixture of rue, Saint-John's-wort, and vervain along its edge. As you do, say these words:

> Mark *I this place with rue, wort, and vervain,*
> *setting a circle that for evil is bane.*

Repeat the words three times as you move around the circle.

Now it is time to prepare the tools of Old Ways witchcraft inside the circle.

Mortar

The mortar is one of the main tools. It represents the womb of the Night Queen and is known as the Life-giver and Death-taker. To consecrate it, anoint the mortar with dew collected on the early morning following the night of a full moon. To do this, wet the index finger on the left hand and then trace the lip of the mortar (three times). Next, rewet the finger and dab it three times inside the mortar (directly center). I recommend collecting dew when it is available and keeping a bottle of it on hand so that you have it as needed.

When anointing the mortar, speak the words of blessing:

I call to Mother womb and ancient tomb,
be blessed by the water of the moon

Pestle

The pestle is the masculine half of the mortar set, and is mated to the mortar as a primary tool in Old World witchcraft. The pestle is also called the Horn-awakener when used for gain and increase. It is known as the Serpent-slumberer when used for decline and dissolving. To consecrate it, wrap a leaf that is wet with morning dew around the tip of the pestle. Slide the wet leaf down the shaft of the pestle and back up to the tip (do this three times).

When anointing the pestle, speak the words of blessing:

I call to Father horn and ancient snake,
blessings of the moon's water to now awake.

Knife

The knife is the harvester, a tool that severs and separates so that something may be collected or gathered. While it is used to cut plants, it is not used to cut anything else in the material world. It is, however, used as a knife to cut a space that allows for the casting of a ritual or magical circle.

To consecrate the knife, anoint the end of the handle and the tip of the blade with dew. Then wet your finger and trace around the hilt three times.

When anointing the knife, speak the words of blessing:

I call to metal and fire's ancient forge,
in moon water blessings flows now the surge.

Wand

The wand is the sign of the master of the Greenwood magic. It links the witch to the inherent power of the plant realm. Trees possess the deepest roots and therefore tap into the greater mysteries and powers of the shadow beneath the earth. To hold the wand is to wield the ancient forces.

To consecrate the wand, wet your finger and anoint the bottom of the wand. Then draw your finger up to the top of the wand. Repeat this three times.

When anointing the wand, speak the words of blessing:

I call to sacred center, bridge of ancient light,
moon water's blessing of black sacred night.

Platter

The platter is used to mark symbols for various rites. The sacred ashes of burned plant materials are sprinkled to cover the face of the platter, which serves as a type of "painting canvas" to mark symbols on. After each use, the ashes are returned to their container. The platter should have no markings on its face. In other words, it should be a solid color, and this needs to contrast against the color of the ash.

As a magical tool, the platter is sometimes referred to as the mirror of the moon. This title is connected to the idea of light reflecting off a pool, pond, or lake. In a mystical sense the symbols etched into the ash are reflections of lunar light, and they pass to and from the moon.

To consecrate the platter, wet your finger with dew and mark an X directly in the center of the plate. Then wet the finger again and trace along the edge of the platter, circling three times.

When anointing the platter, speak the words of blessing:

I call to light's mirror, keeper of the dream,
blessings of the moon's water here and in-between.

Broom

The broom represents the power of the witch to traverse the spirit world. It is the sacred tree in connection with the ruling genius spirit of the dead—the birch. The broom draws together the power of ash, birch, and willow. The ash is the bridge tree connecting material reality with nonmaterial reality. The willow is sacred to Hecate, and as its bark strips bind the sweep to the handle of the broom, it is a reminder of what binds the witch to the Night Queen.

To consecrate the broom, set it on the ground with the sweep end upward. Wet your finger with dew and anoint the end of the handle, then the binding, and finally the tips of the sweep material.

When anointing the broom, speak the words of blessing:

I call to ancient hearth-keeper, stewart of the light,
blessings of the moon's water to traverser of the night.

Branch (Stang)

As noted in chapter four, there are two branches used in Old Ways witchcraft. They are the masculine and feminine stangs. The former is a forked branch with the extending twigs left to symbolize a set of antlers. The latter is a forked branch that is trimmed smooth of any twigs.

The masculine stang is used to create an opening with the perimeter of the ritual or magical circle. It is also used to open portals between the worlds and to represent the forest entity: He of the Deep Wooded Places.

The feminine stang is used to mark the perimeter of the ritual or magical circle. It also serves to represent the presence of the lunar entity: She of the White Round. The feminine stang can also be used to mark out a crossroads pattern on the ground that represents the setting of the crossroads.

When anointing the masculine stang, speak the words of blessing:

> I call to He of the Shadowed Forest Deep,
> blessings of the moon water where sky and branches meet.

When anointing the feminine stang, speak the words of blessing:

> I call to She of the White Round,
> blessings of the moon's water to abound.

Now that we have looked at how to bless the tools in blackness and light, it is time to establish a formal altar for consecrating the ritual and magical tools.

The idea of a formal altar is not technically a concept in Old World witchcraft. The original idea was closer to a work area, and often a fallen tree was used as the place for items for the ritual, but in modern times most practitioners use an altar. I believe that the older view of deity was not one that required veneration, but instead regarded powerful beings as allies that could be persuaded to render aid. Perhaps the definition of "religion" or "religious" differs with Old Ways witches.

Essentially, the altar is the center and focal point that connects to the Hallow, and through this to spirits and deities. It occupies the direct center point of the ritual or magical circle. In this way it symbolizes the Hallow, which stands in the center where material reality and nonmaterial reality meet.

The altar establishes a portal or gateway between the worlds and the inner planes. This is represented by fire, either in the form of a lighted candle or an oil lamp. The flame occupies the center spot. Fire, as an earlier divine image (such as Hestia or Vesta), establishes the presence of divinity within the circle.

A black cloth is used to cover the altar. This represents the procreative blackness from which all things issue forth. As humans we were born from the black space within the womb into the world of light. The sun and moon seemingly rise from the black realm below the earth, which births their light. It is an ancient theme.

Two altar candles representing the Goddess and God are set at the back of the altar and are separated, each placed at the far end of the altar. Along with the center flame, they form the base of a triangle. These represent the principle of manifestation. The color of the Goddess candle is red and the God candle is black. The meaning of these colors is explained as we continue.

Next to the altar candles an image of the Goddess and God can be placed. These figures serve as interfacing devices through which the images link to the concepts they represent. The concept in turn connects with the energy behind it all. It is a type of magical thread connecting energy to a concept that is expressed in a material object.

Between the images of deity is placed a representation of a human skull. This symbolizes the knowledge and wisdom of our spiritual lineage that is preserved and passed on through the Old Ways. A black candle is set on the head of the skull and is lighted for all rituals performed from the Autumn Equinox until the Spring Equinox. A red candle is used from the Spring Equinox until the Autumn Equinox. Black symbolizes the ancestral knowledge retained within shadow and its connection to the realm of the Otherworld. Red symbolizes the ancestral knowledge that flows from the Otherworld to the world of mortals. It is the living river of blood that flows through the generations of witches.

During the course of the year, the color of the skull's candle changes to match either that of the Goddess or God candle. Black represents the secret shadow realm, the deep dark forest, and the mystical journey that leads to the Otherworld. The God is the escort of the dead, who aids in transition.

Red represents the life's blood, the inner pulse that sustains and empowers. Regarding its connection to the Goddess, this current runs through the earth beneath the soil (for she is the giver of life). Red symbolizes the vehicle of life and renewal, which is reflected in the menstrual blood cycle. In the context of the skull figure, red symbolizes the ancient river of blood flowing into the world of the living. It flows from the ancestral memory retained in shadow, which is the source of its wellspring.

In front of the skull a small cauldron is placed on the altar, which contains the sacred stone. The cauldron represents the *Well of the Moon*, which in this context is the womb of the Goddess. Through the Goddess all things are birthed from the Otherworld and are returned to her again. Therefore, the cauldron leads to and from the ancestral knowledge and opens into the realm of shadow. Because of this, it contains the magical essence of transformation. The altar is oriented to the east, meaning that the practitioner is facing east as he or she views the altar.

Consecrating the Tools

The word "consecrate" means to declare or set apart something as sacred. In this regard, the consecration of ritual and magical tools is a way of placing them in a current of special energy. Sacredness applies to something dedicated or devoted exclusively to a single use, purpose, or deity. This separates it from things that are mundane. Mundane applies to anything commonplace. When something becomes mundane, it loses its connection to sacredness.

In Old Ways witchcraft the idea of sacredness is rooted in the concept of reaching out to forces greater than us. It is a means of interacting with spiritual realities that enrich our knowledge and experience. We separate sacredness from the mundane and then we can perceive a special quality. A meadow belongs to the mundane world but can become sacred to us by the way we use it. If we make it a ritual site, then sacredness connects us. If we make it a toxic waste dump, it does not. While creation possesses a sacred nature in the sense that it comes from its divine creators, we can interfere and sever sacredness, or we can act to maintain sacredness. Even our primitive ancestors sensed when something or someplace was sacred or taboo.

To consecrate any of your tools, perform the following. Add three teaspoons of salt to a pot of boiling water, and speak these words:

I purify this fluid essence to expel disharmony to open the entry of sacredness to all that it touches.

Remove the pot from the fire. Using a wooden spoon, dip out the water and then sprinkle the tool (repeating three times). Each tool can be dedicated to a specific entity or usage as you wish. You can customize the assignment by applying the desired name to connect with the specific tool. The traditional assignments are as follows:

> Mortar and pestle: The Hallow
> Feminine stang: She of the White Round
> Masculine stang: He of the Deep Wooded Places
> Wand: He of the Deep Wooded Places
> Knife: Three Daughters of Night
> Platter: The Hallow
> Broom: She of the White Round
> Cauldron: She of the Crossroads
> Ghost Stone: She of the Crossroads

As you sprinkle each tool, speak the following:

With this purifying water, I consecrate this tool in the name of [give name] and dedicate it to [her/his/their] service.

Once the tools are consecrated, treat them with the reverence due any sacred object. None of the tools may be used for non-ritual, non-magical, or non-spiritual purposes. When not being used, keep the tools on an altar or wrapped and put away in a drawer, cabinet, or trunk.

The Book of Ways

In Old World witchcraft there are prescribed methods pertaining to ritual and magical work. Old Ways witches don't believe that only their ways work. Instead, they honor the ways that have always worked. This is founded on the belief of the power of "rootedness" versus contemporary invention. One of the core beliefs in Old World witchcraft is the principle known as "the momentum of the past." Essentially, it means that when something is performed repeatedly in the same way over many generations, it carries a momentum of energy. Something newly invented or created requires time to gain such momentum.

The principle of the momentum of the past demonstrates that the repeating of an ancient act in present time connects to its memory in the past. When the memory is awakened, it "jumps the gap" between past and present; the past memory and the current act join together. This is like the formation and cresting of a wave that pours down upon the shore.

The rituals and procedures in this section are based upon the formation of generational power. Specific keys to the momentum of the past are included with the text. At the core of it all is the enchanted worldview, which is a philosophy underlying all the beliefs and practices of the witch. Among the enchanted forces are those called the *Asthesia* (pronounced As-thay-zah). They correspond to the elementals in modern Wicca and witchcraft but are viewed as primal forces that animate the elemental natures as opposed to being the elementals.

The following entries comprise the basic book of ways in Old World witchcraft. Some are very old concepts and others are modern adaptations if not constructions. It is the spiritual lineage that is important because this connects the ways to currents of energy that flow through time.

1. The Ash Pot

This device holds the ashes of the sacred tree or trees, and these will vary for each witch. Each witch feels her or his own connection to a tree, which can be regarded as the patroness or patron of the witch. This tree is selected for creating sacred ash. All parts of the tree are harvested: a bit of root, bark, limb, and leaf. These are burned together on the night of the full moon.

The ashes are collected and put into a pot for later use. Over time, new ash will be needed to resupply the pot. The ashes are used in conjunction with the platter to create the symbols and sigils of the witches' magical art. In the art of witchcraft a symbol represents a thing, while a sigil is regarded as the presence of the thing itself.

2. The Platter

The platter is a simple plate that is light in color and has no design imprinted on it. Ideally, the platter should be white (or silver). Sacred ash from the pot is sprinkled over it, completely covering the face. A fingertip is used to draw in the ash. This reveals the color of the plate beneath the ash, and by contrast the symbol appears. After every use the ash is returned to the pot, and the platter is wiped clean.

Before using the platter for this purpose, the symbol of the Hallow is drawn in the ash. The statement is made that the platter is dedicated to the Hallow, and then the ash is returned to the pot. See the Book of Calls for the symbol, and the Book of Magic for using the platter.

3. Dust Pots

Dust is an old magical term for herbs that are ground into powder. The dust is kept in a small pot, jar, or bottle. Each container holds the dust of a single type of plant. However, combinations can be made such as the mixture of rue, vervain, and Saint-John's-wort used to sprinkle around the perimeter of a ritual or magical circle, which in Old World witchcraft is known as the Round.

When making dust pots, be sure to label them in order not to confuse matters. Be careful when opening a dust pot, or removing dust, so that you do not inhale any of the powder. Many of the witchcraft herbs contain toxic and poisonous elements.

4. The Rose Brew

A sacred brew can be used for offerings when summoning spirits or calling upon entities. It is to be used sparingly at times of special need. On the first night of the waxing moon (first appearance of the crescent), take a large handful of red rose petals and place them in a small jar (no more than eight ounces). Fill the jar with a high-quality alcohol (Everclear is ideal, but vodka will do). Leave the mixture for one full cycle of the moon. Shake the bottle every third day.

When the moon cycle is complete, strain the liquid through cheesecloth until the petals are cleared. Bury them near your herb garden. Bottle the Rose Brew and keep it out of sunlight until usage.

5. The Ghost Stone

A dedicated stone is used to work with spirits of the dead in a variety of ways. The most common use is to quell a haunting or bind a wayward spirit from causing harm. The use of a stone to confine spirits of the dead is one of the concepts of the headstone in a graveyard, but in mundane use, they are simply markers by which to remember a deceased loved one.

In Old World witchcraft the Ghost Stone has three uses. One is to bring peace to a haunting spirit. Another use is to draw the spirit into the stone so that it can be taken elsewhere. The third is to temporarily hold the spirit in the stone for oracle use or ancestral connection. See the Book of Magic section for instructions.

6. The Witches' Broom

This is perhaps the least realized of all the witches' tools. It is used to sweep energy and to draw power to the witch from the three realms: Above, Below, and In-between. Its ability to access these realms is a metaphor for flight, and in this sense the witch rides the broom when she or he meets the three worlds.

The technique for using the broom is greatly detailed in my book *The Cauldron of Memory*, but I will give the basics here. To draw power, hold the broom vertically and raise your arms up to full extension. Envision yourself as a tree touching the heavens. Lower the broom down slowly as though you are pulling something down from the sky, which indeed you are. Then bring the broom handle sharply down to the ground with force. When the end of the broom impacts with the ground, close your eyes and envision deep roots extending from the broom far down into Shadow.

After a few moments pull the handle back up slowly. When your elbows are level with your rib cage, turn the broom horizontal with the sweep pointing right, and then turn it the left. This aligns you and the broom with the forces of the three realms. Turning the broom to the right opens the portals to the realms, and to the left closes them.

7. Setting the Round

The concept of the Round is similar to the idea of the ritual circle in modern Wicca and witchcraft, but there are several differences, including the absence of "Watchers," or "Grigori," who are called to the quarters. In essence, the Round is derived from the imagery of the full moon. Because of its sacred connection to Old World witchcraft, the image of the full moon is etched into the earth so that we can be within it in both a physical and spiritual sense. In this light, the ritual act of "drawing down the moon" is literally drawing it on the earth.

To begin setting the Round, take you broom and ritually sweep the physical area where the circle will be drawn. Then, use the end of the feminine stang to etch the perimeter of the circle in a clockwise manner. Once completed, use the broom to sweep the air above the perimeter. Ideally, you will begin in the east and work around the circle clockwise until you return to the east.

It is time now to place the altar directly center inside the circle. Arrange it as prescribed earlier in this chapter. Then place the four bowls of the Asthesia at each cardinal point of the Round: east, south, west, north. In the eastern bowl place three feathers. The southern bowl contains a lighted red candle. The western bowl is filled with clean water, and the northern bowl contains newly dug earth. While placing each bowl, call upon its Asthesia to empower it and establish the elemental force (see Book of Calls).

After placing the bowls, return to the altar. Light the center flame and call to the Hallow (see Book of Calls). Next, light the candle on the left and call to *She of the White Round* (see Book of Calls). Then light the candle on the right and call to *He of the Deep Wooded Places* (see Book of Calls). Finish by lighting the candle on top of the skull, and then call to *She of the Crossroads* (see Book of Calls).

Take your wand in the left hand and pass it three times through the center flame on the altar. As you do so, speak these words:

I draw from the Hallow.

Then pass the wand three times through the flame on the skull while saying:

I call to memory within the Shadow.

Next, hold the wand over the left altar candle and say:

From She of the White Round,
I pass virtue into the circle.

Hold the wand over the right altar candle and say:

From He of the Deep Wooded Places,
I pass virtue into the circle.

Go immediately to the eastern perimeter and switch the wand to your right hand. Point it down at the circle's edge, raise your left hand up into the air, and then walk along the edge from the east and back again. As you walk the Round, say these words:

As above, so it is below,
Round is formed from head to toe.
Enclosing all, an Orb of light,
I set the Round and seal the site.

Take your pouch containing the mixture of crushed rue, vervain, and Saint-John's-wort, and sprinkle the blend along the perimeter edge of the circle. Begin at the east and return. As you move along the circle's edge, repeat the incantation:

As above, so it is below,
Round is formed from head to toe.
Enclosing all, an Orb of light,
I set the Round and seal the site.

All that remains now is to return to the altar and make the ritual knoll. To do so, ring a bell three times, and then firmly tap the altar three times with the base of the wand. End by declaring:

The Round is set.

8. Rite of the Blood Thorn

The Old Ways witch belongs to a spiritual lineage that connects her or him to the shadow-memory of all witches from the past. It is an old teaching that the force known as Shadow contains the memory of everything absorbed into the earth. From this rises the belief that the knowledge of witches who are now dead can be tapped within their collective consciousness. This is called listening to the whispers of those in shadow.

To inherit this lineage requires a formal ritual known as the rite of the blood thorn. The simplest method involves the pricking of the left hand in the area known in palmistry as the Mount of Venus. This is the "meaty" area of the hand connected to the thumb. Earlier we noted that Venus was originally a goddess of gardens and that witches were originally connected to plant knowledge. Elements of the blood thorn rite are vestiges of this ancient connective concept.

The following items are needed for the ritual: one rose thorn, a chalice filled with red wine, the mortar and pestle, knife, and staff. Set these up at a crossroads, preferably in a rural area away from the energy of a city. Etch the witch's mark into the soil, and push the blade of the knife through its center and down into the soil. Next, use the end of your staff to mark a circle around this area (large enough for you to work within the space).

Facing east, stand over the knife with your legs spread, handle pointing directly at your groin. Raise the staff up in your right hand and the chalice of wine in your left. In this posture, give the call to She of the Crossroads from the Book of Calls:

> I call to She of the Crossroads,
> Gatekeeper, Path Opener,

She of the Triple names,
Blessed trine,
Shine your light to reveal the parting,
Shed your light to reveal the ways.

Set the staff aside, and slowly pour out half of the wine over the knife handle so that it soaks into the soil. Then, looking at the witch's mark, use the bottom of your staff to drum on the earth nine times, in groups of three beats: 1-2-3 [pause], 1-2-3 [pause], 1-2-3 [stop]. While drumming, speak the following words:

I stir and summon, and shadow call,
one in present joined now to all.
Past and present affix our kind,
Flow shadow memory into my mind.

Take the rose thorn and prick your hand as prescribed. Squeeze out three drops of your blood into the chalice so that it mixes with the wine. Next, slowly pour some wine over the knife handle, while being careful to save a little for mixing later in the rite. As you pour the wine, say:

I call upon She of the Thorn-blooded Rose.

Set the chalice aside. Next, cup the knife handle between both hands and speak these words:

I summon now the spirit of the Thorn-blooded Rose,
draw what the witches' ancestral memory knows,
my blood calls through your mystical breath,
grant now the sacred union that I request.

Immediately following the words of summoning, pull the knife from the ground. Then use the blade to scrap the soil containing the witch's mark into a pile. Next use the side of the blade to scoop the soil into the mortar. This is transference of the collected energy from shadow into the vessel. Once you have completed this, scrape both sides of the blade against the inner lip of the mortar. Next, tap the side of the blade three times on the edge of the mortar, saying:

Blood of life, whisper of shadow, enter in and outward flow.

Set the knife aside, and then pour the remaining wine into the mortar. Using the fingers of the left hand, mix the wine and soil, and then scoop up a small portion of the mixture. Repeat this for each anointing that follows.

Mark the tops of both feet, the back of each wrist, the heart area, and both sides of the neck. The anointed areas are points where the beating of the heart can be felt. Once all areas have been marked with the soil and wine mixture, there is one last call to give. Stand with both feet together, knife in the right hand and staff in the left. Raise both arms up and give the call:

I am a Thorn-blooded witch of the Ways.
Roots beneath, hear me,
Shadow below, know me.
Branches above, connect me,
for in-between I stand
as a Thorn-blooded witch of the ways.

This concludes the rite. Clean the site and retrieve the items. Return home and bathe. At some point you will want to obtain a ring with a red stone to mark yourself as one of the Thorn-blooded witches. The ring is always worn on the left hand.

9. The Black Moon Rite

The ritual of the Black Moon is intended to connect you with the force known as Shadow. In essence, Shadow is a force that holds memory and can impart this to the witch. It is the vault of ancestral wisdom and knowledge. Every living thing that died and was buried in soil passed the energy of its experience into the earth. The energy of each deed is absorbed into the land. This is why places have a feel to them. The land remembers; places remember.

After sunset, when night rules the sky, the presence of Shadow rises from the earth. This is the spiritual blackness, a term you may think is contradictive. But when we consider that the color black is the presence of all colors mixed together, the concept becomes clear. Black is everything, and is the potential lurking in the un-manifest. In sunlight things appear as they are; it is the perception of finite reality as viewed in the light. In the blackness we encounter unlimited possibilities. Anything might be there, and therefore anything is possible as a result.

It is at night that spirits of the plants most often communicate with the witch. This is one of the reasons why witchcraft plants are traditionally harvested at night. From an esoteric perspective, Shadow emerges from the earth and pools around plants in the blackness of night. This increases the presence of Shadow in a plant that is harvested at night. The Black Moon is the ideal time, for not even the light of the moon disturbs the black.

The rite of the Black Moon can be performed on any or all of the three nights during which the moon is unseen in the night sky. However, each moonless night is associated with one of the Three

Daughters of Night. They are known as the Lady of Shadow, Lady of Blood, and Lady of Bone. This is the order assigned to the three nights of the black moon.

The Lady of Shadow brings forth its power from beneath the earth, and with it comes the potentiality of all things (the very definition of magic itself). In Shadow resides the memory of all it has been absorbed from the living beings whose material form dissolved into the earth. The Lady of Shadow brings this nature forth as the purity of potentiality. Through her, all things are made possible.

The Lady of Blood receives the emanation of the occult properties placed into her hands by the Lady of Shadow. Through the Lady of Blood this power enters into the world of the living and can be utilized by the mortal witch. In turn, the force is then passed from the Lady of Blood into the hands of the Lady of Bone. Here, it is retained and preserved, taking on the new experiences of the living generation. The Lady of Bone then sinks into Shadow where what she possesses passes back to the Lady of Shadow. This begins the next cycle of passing and receiving.

Prepare for the Black Moon ritual by assembling the following: a small cauldron, a bottle of red wine, a handful of white flour, and three black candles. Take these to a crossroads at night; the best times are at 9:00 p.m. or midnight. Orient the work so that you face west. The ritual is as follows:

1. Place the three black candles next to each other in a row, separated by a hand's width. In front of each candle, from left to right, place one of the objects. Beginning at the left, place the cauldron, then the bottle of wine, and finally the mound of flour. In front of the cauldron, mark a serpent in the soil. Likewise, in front of the wine bottle, etch a heart into the soil. Lastly, in front of the

flour, mark a bone in the soil (like the figure of one of the crossbones typically shown with a skull).

2. Starting to the left and working to the right, light each candle and evoke each of the Three Daughters of Night.

I call to the Lady of Shadow,
bringer and wielder of Shadow,
bestower of the mystic cauldron,
revealer of the teachings,
in the black of night.

I call to the Lady of Blood,
stirrer of the cauldron,
tender of the ancestral river,
flowing in through our veins.

I call to the Lady of the Bone,
keeper of the Cauldron of Memory,
preserver of all that was, is, and shall be.
Gatherer of the scattered bones.

3. Pour some of the wine into the cauldron and then add the flour. Lift up the cauldron, presenting it to the night sky and say:

I am a Thorn-blooded witch of the ways,
seer of the black sacred night and the bright blessed day.
I call to the Shadow around and below,
reveal your veiled mysteries and to me bestow.

4. Arrange the black candles into a triangle formation with the center large enough to contain the cauldron. Set the cauldron there, and then stir the contents with the fingers of your left hand. As you stir the mixture, speak these words:

Night, keeper of all secrets,
black moon veiled above,
mother of the Three,
draw forth the Shadow into this blend.

5. Withdraw your fingers from the cauldron, taking with them some of the mixture. Hold your fingers in front of you over the cauldron, and say these words:

From the river of blood and the banks of bone,
rises the black moon
with a light that is not shown.

6. Place the mixture on your fingers into your mouth and consume that portion. This is the sacred meal of the Black Moon.

7. Stand for a few moments with your feet together and your arms extended above your head. Envision yourself to be tree. Sense your arms as the branches, your body as the trunk, and your feet as roots. Envision roots going from your feet deep into the earth. Envision that they dip into the deep pool of black far below you. Stay receptive in this state for a while. Listen for the whispers of those who dwell in Shadow.

8. Sit comfortably on the ground with both palms pressed against the earth. Take in a deep breath and then exhale slowly. Envision the energy of your breath passing down through your arms and into the earth. Repeat this three times.

[This is an exchange of energy with the shadow, for nothing may be received without something being given, and nothing may be given without something being received. This is the witch law.]

9. Conclude the rite by pouring out the wine onto the soil. Do this as a libation to the Three Daughters of Night. Then dig a small hole and pour out the contents of the cauldron into it, and then fill the hole back in with soil.

10. Retrieve your items and leave the area clean of debris. The rite is ended. Return home and look to your dreams. Shadow will come to you from the plant spirits, and you will be taught in your sleep.

10. Full Moon Rite (for a Coven)

The ritual, performed beneath the full moon, has several purposes. It is a time to "recharge" through the light of the moon and to connect with Otherworld forces. As noted earlier in the book, references to witch gatherings depict them as times to commune with the dead. This is still a time to venerate those who came before. The ritual also draws the presence of the Old Ones, which can be viewed as deity if one wishes.

In Old World witchcraft there is no formal priestess or priest role. Instead, for group rituals, the female facilitator is known as the *Sacerdotessa* (pronounced sah-chur-doh-tessa), which means "one who keeps sacredness" (in this case, within the ritual). The male counterpart is known as the *Sacerdote* (pronounced sah-chur-doh-tay). These titles are ancient, but their incorporation into witchcraft rituals is modern.

Before beginning the ritual, prepare the Round and the altar as prescribed. Once this is completed, the ritual can begin. The ritual is structured as follows:

1. Standing at the altar, facing east, the Sacerdotessa speaks the opening words:

    On this night of the Full Moon,
    we gather once more beneath the sacred light.

In the presence of She of the White Round,
And He of the Deep Wooded Places.

Coven replies: "As it was in the time of our beginning, so is it now, so shall it be!"

2. The Sacerdote gives each coven member a red candle. The Sacerdotessa goes to each circle quarter and places a white candle, lighting each one in turn.

3. The Sacerdotessa and Sacerdote each take a red candle from the altar and light them from the eastern candle. Once lighted, the candles are carried around the circle. Each time a quarter is approached, the bearer of the candle says:

To the Round, I add my light.

Coven members move in turn, lighting their candles and moving about the circle behind the facilitators. They also speak the words at each quarter: "To the Round, I add my light." Upon returning to the east quarter, the candles are blown out, symbolically returning the flame back to the eastern candle.

4. At the altar, the Sacerdotessa places her hands, palms down, over the altar, and says:

Let us now give offerings to the Old Ones.

The offerings are handed out to the coven members who take them to the east quarter. Singing, drumming, and chanting accompany this period of making offerings. After the offerings are all in place, the coven forms along the perimeter of the circle.

5. The Sacerdotessa fills the small cauldron on the altar with water and then holds up the sacred stone, saying:

Look now upon the sacred stone of our coven,
keeper of the memories and spirit of our ways.
Through it we are never parted,
Through it, nothing is ever forgotten.

She then places the sacred stone inside the cauldron, and goes to the west to set the cauldron at this quarter. After a moment, the Sacerdote retrieves it and carries the stone over to the east quarter where he dries it with a cloth.

6. Next, the stone is passed clockwise once around the circle to each coven member who holds it for a moment, connecting with the inner spirit. Before passing the stone, the coven member says:

I am a Thorn-blooded witch of the ways,
I join with the spirit of the sacred stone here,
I join all of my kin.

When the stone is passed to the next person, the person passing says:

Together are we.
[and this is repeated back to the giver]

7. When the stone returns to the east quarter, it is placed on the circle's edge and left until the close of the circle.

8. The Sacerdotessa goes to the altar with the sacred stone and addresses the coven:

We are one in the Round,
and we have shared the touch of the sacred stone of our coven.

Coven replies: "Yes, we are one." (Members embrace each other and afterward hold hands together in the circle.)

9. The Sacerdote addresses coven:

There are others now to call to the Round,
for they are kin
and belong with us this night in spirit.

10. The Sacerdotessa lifts the skull from the altar. She holds it above her head and addresses the coven:

I call to the spirits of our ancestors,
I call to our loved ones now departed,
I call to the memories of all witches in Shadow.
[pause]
Come pass from the west for this night,
And join us in the Round once more.

11. The Sacerdote takes the masculine stang and goes to the west quarter followed by the Sacerdotessa carrying the skull. He holds up the stang to the west and says:

I call to She of the Crossroads,
who aids all enchantments
and befriends the witch,
be now of favor and open the western gates
so we may have union this night with those on the other side.

Coven chants: "rukus roykus mitha-sis ulay-a-thess, ala-rey moritta, un naw maya-thuss."

12. The Sacerdote inserts the branch end of the stang into the western wall of the Round, moves it from left to right (as though parting a curtain), and then lays it on the ground (partly breeching the circle's edge).

13. The Sacerdotessa brings a reed basket containing "birch dolls" to the west quarter and stands facing east.

14. Coven members pass by the Sacerdotessa who tosses them a birch doll. Members catch the doll and then move off to form a circle along the edge of the Round.

15. When everyone is in place, drumming and dancing begins. The dolls are held up during the dance and coven members toss them to each other, back and forth, and all around. This is the Dance of the Dead.

16. The Sacerdote signals an end to the dancing, and all music stops. Coven members applaud the festivity.

17. The Sacerdotessa announces it is time for the feast. Everyone settles into a comfortable place as the food is served. This is the time of social connection. The birch dolls are kept present so that the spirits can join in.

18. At a chosen time the Sacerdote announces the end of the feast. He then addresses the coven:

    The time has come now for our spirit kin to return.
    I call upon She of the Crossroads to gather them now.
    All return now to the Other Land, all return now.
    In the name of She of the Crossroads,
    All return now.

19. The Sacerdotessa takes the reed basket to the west quarter (walking counterclockwise) and stands facing west.

20. Coven members walk to the west (moving counterclockwise) as they carry the birch dolls to the reed basket. The Sacerdotessa collects them in the basket.

21. When the basket is filled, it is attached to the end of the stang held by the Sacerdote. He then passes them out of

the circle through the west and sets them on the ground.
The Sacerdote pulls the stang back into the circle. He
then points the branch end to the west and swings it
from right to left (as in closing a curtain). To finalize,
he lowers the stang to meet the ground inside the circle.
After a pause, the stang is returned to stand at its quarter.

22. The Sacerdotessa goes to the altar and extinguishes the
flame on the skull, and addresses the coven:

*The Gates to the Land of the Dead are closed, and all have
returned. We have honored the departed, our ancestors,
and our witch kin with dancing and feasting. None are
forgotten, nothing is ever forgotten.*

Coven replies: "As it was in the time of our beginning, so
is it now, so shall it be!"

23. The Sacerdote announces that the ritual has come to a
close. Coven members prepare to release the Round.

24. The Asthesia are released by deactivating the forces at
each quarter bowl. Beginning at the east, and moving
counterclockwise, the Sacerdote places a cloth over each
bowl (extinguishing the candle at the south before placing the cloth). As each cloth is laid, he speaks the words
of release:

For air: *I release the Aesthesia of air to carry off its
attachment to the Round.*
For earth: *I release the Aesthesia of earth to crumble its
attachment to the Round.*
For water: *I release the Aesthesia of water to recede from
its attachment to the Round.*
For fire: *I release the Aesthesia of fire to cease its
attachment to the Round.*

25. The Sacerdotessa speaks to the Old Ones for attending the ritual:

Old Ones, in goodwill we bid you farewell,
the branches call you home,
the night sky reaches to embrace you,
and so we part until the White Round unites us once again.
[left and right altar candles are now extinguished]

Coven calls out: "Hail and Farewell!"

26. The Sacerdote speaks to the Hallow:

In goodwill we release our draw upon the Hallow.
In withdrawing, all things here return to their former state.
We stand once again in the world of mortal kind,
And the Hallow abides where all worlds meet.
[center flame on altar is extinguished]

Coven calls out: "We stand again in the realm of mortal kind!"

27. The Sacerdotessa makes the final announcement:

The Round is lifted and released,
the night revels are now deceased,
depart in peace without a sound
till we meet again in the sacred Round!
[This ends the ritual.]

The Book of Calls

The ancient idea of magic is that something can be summoned through sound. The primary method was to sing, and later this became the idea of speaking in rhyme. This is evidenced in the word *incantation*, which means to chant. Chanting is an old specific form of singing and forming song. Over time incantation became the speaking of words within a spell or ritual. Often the words were spoken with a specific tonal quality; one example is the Gregorian chants, which have a droning quality to their sound.

In addition to the concept of incantation, the magical arts also include the words invocation and evocation. To *invoke* is to call something to manifest within a person, place, or thing. The key is that invocation directs something to inhabit in some way. The word *evocation* means to call something to show itself; it is the outward manifestation versus the inner manifestation meant by invocation.

Old Ways witches often use the word *call* in place of invocation or evocation. The intent of the call, and what is being asked, determines the desired inner or outer manifested request. In other words, is the call asking something to appear? Or is it requesting something to instill (as with an inner presence)? Words such as "I call forth . . ." and "I call to enter in . . ." all indicate and direct an evocation or invocation.

All calls are preceded by the acclamation of the witch, which announces her or his spiritual lineage and the personal connection to the three mystical realms. In doing so, the witch stands with feet together fully planted in a posture of strength. The wand, or stang, is held in the left hand and both hands are raised upward. The call is given as follows:

> *I am a Thorn-blooded witch of the Ways.*
> *Roots below and branches above,*
> *and in-between I stand,*
> *a wielder of shadow to and fro.*

The Calls that follow are methods of summoning an entity.

To Call: *She of the Crossroads*

The entity known as "She of the Crossroads" possesses a triformis nature. She is separated into aspects called the Lady of Shadow, the Lady of Blood, and the Lady of Bone. These are also known as the Three Daughters of Night (when called as separated aspects). Each daughter is respectively connected to a color: black, red, and white. The black color of the Lady of Shadow associates her with the force of shadow and with the Underworld/Otherworld. Red, in its connection to the Lady of Blood, symbolizes the living river of blood flowing through each generation (passing to the current keepers of family bloodlines). The white color of the Lady of Bone represents the ancestral memory that remains throughout time.

Each of these Ladies is envisioned holding a sacred object and wearing a hooded robe that matches her symbolic color. The Lady of Shadows holds a coiled serpent between her hands just below her navel. A heart is held by the Lady of Blood and is cupped with both hands below the navel. The Lady of Bone holds a human skull in the same fashion. The Lady of Shadow "brings forth," and what emanates from her then flows into the river of blood, which in turn is passed to bone. These are the living inner mysteries of She of the Crossroads.

The entity is called for one of two purposes. She is always evoked whenever any venture, ritual, relationship, or decision is going to be developed or entertained.

As humans we are forced into the world through birth, and forced out of the world by death. Life is the only choice we have in our hands. Through the aid of She of the Crossroads, we can make conscious and more informed choices.

The secondary purpose for calling upon her is when the need or desire to communicate with ancestors (or any spirits of the dead) arises. She is an ally as well as a go-between or mediator. She can also be of aid when dealing with wayward spirits, hauntings, and things of this general nature. By proper request, she can connect you to anyone that dwells in spirit form.

Prior to evoking this entity, you must prepare a few things. On a platter, place equal sections of grain, fruit, and white flour. Also select a red wine. These are your food offerings at the crossroads. You will also need to place three black beans into a red pouch. The last items you need to assemble are three candles, one black, one red, and one white. Once you have these, locate a crossroads. This is anywhere three or four roads intersect. Ideally, the crossroads should be located in a rural setting, but you can use one within a city area if need be. As a last resort, you can use the feminine stang to etch out a crossroads in the earth. In this case, you will afterwards stand the branch upright in the center of the intersection.

Go to your crossroads at either 9:00 p.m. or at midnight as these times are of particular sacredness to Her. Facing west, place the food offerings and the container of wine on the intersection of the roads. Surround the offerings with the three candles, forming a triangle with their placement. The candle in front of you is black, to your right is the red one, and to the left is the white candle.

To begin evoking She of the Crossroads, light all three candles in the order of their original placement, and then pour out a portion of the wine directly in the center of the triangle. Extend your arms out in front of you as though reaching for something. Then place your hands together side by side with palms facing upward. This is the posture of giving and receiving, for both feelings must be held in the mind, body, and spirit when working with magic and its associated beings.

When you feel ready, begin the evocation of She of the Crossroads:

> *I call to She of the Crossroads,*
> *Gatekeeper, Path Opener,*
> *She of the Triple names,*
> *Blessed trine,*
> *Shine your light to reveal division,*
> *Shed your light to reveal the ways.*
> *I call to She of the Crossroads who commands silence*
> *when secret mysteries are performed,*
> *I summon you.*
> *Night, faithful keeper of my secrets amid the stars, I call to*
> *   you.*
> *She of the Crossroads knows all my designs,*
> *and aids the incantations and the craft of the witches, I*
> *   summon you.*
> *I call to She of the Crossroads,*
> *She who supplies witches with powerful herbs,*
> *night-wandering queen, I summon you.*
> *She of the Crossroads,*
> *look kindly now upon my intention*
> *and manifest my desire.*
> *[state your request]*

To Call: She of the White Round

The entity known as She of the White Round is intimately connected with the phases of the moon. She is the closest idea of a goddess within Old World witchcraft and is similar to the concept of one in the Wiccan model. For simplicity, in this section I will refer to her as the Goddess instead of her older title.

The Goddess manifests through the light of moon, but always in connection with trees. It is the moon seen through branches that denotes her presence. When the moon is seen in any other setting, it is considered to be her sacred light but not the Goddess herself.

In imagery the Goddess only takes on the resemblance of human form when the moon is full. She is envisioned as being within the orb, where she kneels and extends her hands outward to meet its curved edges. In this light, the Goddess appears only once each month to her witches in this manifest form.

The Goddess may be called whenever viewed through the branches of the trees. If no trees are present, then the masculine stang is placed so that the moon is seen through the "antlers" of the stang. From a mystical perspective, the Goddess descends through the bridge of the tree branches or the stang branch. This is why the branch seen against the backdrop of the full moon is important.

To begin calling the Goddess when the moon is full, view the moon against tree branches. Place offerings of white objects such as shells along with food and wine. Fruit and almonds are preferred along with pastry.

When you are ready to begin, give the call to She of the White Round:

> I call to She of the White Round who commands the Night
> when secret mysteries are performed,
> I summon you.
> She of the White Round, bearer of souls in her care,
> Keeper of the Cycle of Life and Death,
> From your cauldron do all things issue forth
> and return again.
> I call to She of the White Round,

look kindly now upon my intention
and manifest my desire.
[state your request]

To Call: The Three Daughters of the Night

The Triformis entity known as the Three Daughters of Night is an aspect of She of the Crossroads. However, in practice, they are most effective when called upon individually or as a triple-natured entity not equated with She of the Crossroads.

The Three Daughters of Night are known separately as the Lady of Shadow, the Lady of Blood, and the Lady of Bones. Each one holds a sacred object in respective order: a serpent, a heart, a femur bone. These represent their inner mystery connection to the realm of Shadow.

When called together, three black candles are lighted side by side at the crossroads. A small cauldron, a bottle of red wine, and a handful of white flour are placed in order from left to right in front of the candles. With these items in place, begin your call to the Three Daughters of Night:

> *I call to the Three Daughters of Night,*
> *you who are bearers of the Shadow,*
> *keepers of the ancient memories,*
> *weavers of the days of mortal kind.*
> *[state your request]*

If you wish, you can call each Daughter individually:

> *I call to the Lady of Shadow,*
> *bringer and wielder of Shadow,*
> *bestower of the mystic cauldron,*

revealer of the teachings
in the black of night.

I call to the Lady of Blood,
stirrer of the cauldron,
tender of the ancestral river
flowing in through our veins.

I call to the Lady of the Bone,
keeper of the Cauldron of Memory,
preserver of all that was, is, and shall be.
Gatherer of the scattered bones.

To Call: He of the Deep Wooded Places

The entity known as He of the Deep Wooded Places is intimately connected to the dense forest. He is the primal spirit of the wooded places who holds together the consciousness of the primeval (untouched by human ways). He is the closest idea of a god in Old Ways witchcraft. For simplicity, I will refer to him in this section as the "God."

The God exists within the woods, and his consciousness is held within the many branches. In this light, the mind of the God is linked to all things through the vast network of branches. When he chooses to appear in a single form, the God takes on the shape of a large stag with mighty antlers. These antlers maintain his connection to the tree branches. It is rare to see the God in humanoid form, but when this happens, he appears with twig branches extended like antlers from his head.

Before calling the God, prepare some offerings in advance. Traditionally, these include the fruits and nuts of the woodlands along with some honey. Mead may also be added as an offering. The God is always called in or near the woods. When this is not possible, place his stang and face north when viewing it. The offerings go at the base of the stang. When all is ready, speak the words of calling:

> *I call to He of the Deep Wooded Places,*
> *Catcher of day and night,*
> *Usher of Life and Death.*
> *He of the Deep Wooded Places*
> *knows all that is seen in light and veiled in shadow.*
> *You who provide sanctuary and safety in the Hidden Places,*
> *I call to you.*
> *He of the Deep Wooded Places,*
> *Look kindly now upon my intention,*
> *And manifest my desire.*
> [state your request]

To Call: The Hallow

The Hallow is an old concept that retains the idea of an ancient center of equilibrium. It is unchanged by anything it has ever had contact with, whether human, Faery, angelic, or any other race of beings. No theology, religion, or spiritual system has ever influenced its existence.

The Hallow stands between the material reality and non-material reality. It is neither, and it makes it possible for both dimensions to interact without collapsing either one. The Hallow emanates energy between realities, and a portion of it can be drawn for magical and ritual use. This energy brings the same essence of equilibrium to any act of magic or ritual, which quells any conflict therein related to the idea of what is real and what is imaginary. In the Hallow, nothing exists or does not exist, for the Hallow buffers any attempt to define, conform, or take an empirical approach.

You can call to the Hallow to find a place of meeting with it in your mind, body, and spirit. This is accomplished by gazing upon the symbol of the Hallow (see symbols in the Book of Magic) for a few moments. Next, you begin making a "humming" sound like that of the bees. The humming is interrupted three times as you speak the words of calling:

> I call to the Hallow,
> the center of purity,
> the enduring unchangeable.
> I call to the Hallow,
> suspend disbelief and belief
> so that all things are as they be.
> I call to the Hallow
> To bring me equilibrium,
> balance, and harmony.

To Call: The Asthesia

The Asthesia are the conscious primal forces of the magical elements known as earth, air, fire, and water. In this regard, they are not the elements; instead they are the animators. Through the occult principle of "like attracts like," the Asthesia are evoked by working with the material forms of the elemental natures.

To prepare calling the Asthesia, set a bowl at each of the four quarters of your round (the ritual circle). In the northern bowl place freshly dug soil. In the eastern bowl, place three bird feathers. In the southern bowl, set a lighted red candle. The western bowl is filled with water.

The Asthesia of air transmit through the wind, and those of fire transform one thing into another through flames. The Asthesia of water bring forth movement through flowing liquid, and those of earth establish form through cohesion. Together they transmit the concept of the round, transform it from imagination to envisioned, move it from the astral form, and establish it through cohesion within material reality.

To call the Asthesia of air, fan the feathers against the ground and then above your head, as you speak the words of calling:

> *I call the Asthesia of air,*
> *come and send forth my intention.*

To call the Asthesia of fire, light a red candle and place your left palm over the flame (close enough to feel the heat but not so close as to burn your skin). Then speak the words of calling:

> *I call the Asthesia of fire,*
> *come and cause the change of my intention.*

To call the Asthesia of water, cup some water in your hands and then allow it to trickle back into the bowl. Repeat this as you speak the words of calling:

> *I call the Asthesia of water,*
> *come and bring movement to flow my intention.*

To call the Asthesia of earth, pour some soil into your hands and compress it between your palms, then speak the words of calling:

> *I call the Asthesia of earth,*
> *come and bring solid form to my intention.*

The Book of Magic

In Old World witchcraft, magic is an energy or force that is attached to all things. The Art of Magic is the means through which this energy is gathered, fashioned, and directed for use in spell casting, ritual, or any work requiring the magical forces. In a more formal expression, some people say that magic is the manifestation of personal will or desire, but this is the end result of applying magic, and is not magic itself (in terms of what it is without human usage).

As previously noted, magical outcomes are connected to human consciousness, which is divided into the Guardian Mind and the Way-Shower. Earlier we saw that the conscious mind rejects the idea of magic as something real and effective. The subconscious is depicted as not acknowledging any lasting form (and therefore undermining the idea of manifestation). Each from their unique perspective makes magic a questionable concept.

In order to realize the existence of magic, the two forms of consciousness we possess must meet and create a third consciousness. It is this third and "shared" consciousness that allows us to draw material and nonmaterial realities together into harmonious existence. The result is a place "in-between," in which there is no objection to magic and what it can accomplish.

The primary tool of the witches' art is the mortar and pestle. It is used to cast spells, commune with the Plant Realm spirits, and draw from the Hallow. Before you begin working with the mortar and pestle, they must first be activated in the traditional manner.

To activate the mortar: Point the head of the pestle down and lower it into the mortar. Begin moving it around in a clockwise fashion while speaking these words:

Seed to earth
Earth to root
Root to sprout
Sprout to leaf
Leaf to bud
Bud to flower
Flower to fruit
Fruit to seed
Seed to earth

Now hold the mortar between your hands and continue speaking:

Womb at the center of all things,
Shaper, transformer, and birther of all,
Hold or free spirits that come to the call,
Life-giver, Death-taker,
Stone Carver, Dream Maker,
I turn the wheel, then to show
And what I spin, it now is so.

To activate the pestle, set it upright in the mortar with the head of the pestle on the top end. Holding it in place, speak these words:

Tree at the center of all things,
Tower from where enchantment sings,
Thresher, dream churner, joiner of all,
Sound for the spirits to come at my call.

The mortar and pestle are now fully activated and ready for magical, ritual, and spiritual use.

Basic spell casting with the mortar and pestle is very simple but powerful. It involves basic manipulations of the pestle inside the mortar. This consists of two motions. One is a tapping back and forth to keep a meter that accompanies incantations. The other motion is "circling" the pestle inside the mortar against its wall. This can be done with the mortar upright (mouth facing up) or on its side (mouth facing to the right or left). The basic function is to call something you desire or to banish anything that is unwanted or troublesome.

Mortar and pestle—The Calling

To perform the spell, begin by placing the mortar on its side. The pestle is inserted inside the mortar and rotated clockwise against the edge of the mortar. Begin moving slowly and then speed up the motion. Say the incantation and then pause to state your desire. Next, repeat the incantation (for a total of three rounds).

> *Turn the Wheel*
> *Set the task*
> *Bring to me*
> *The thing I ask*
> [state intent]

Once the incantations have been completed, hold the mortar in one hand and the pestle in the other. Shake them off at each cardinal point (east, south, west, north) and you say:

> *Go now to the four winds and return with my desire*
> *fulfilled.*

Mortar and pestle—Sending Away

To begin the spell, place the mortar on its side. The pestle is inserted inside the mortar and rotated counterclockwise against the edge of the mortar. Begin moving slowly and then speed up the motion. Say the incantation and then pause to state your desire. Next, repeat the incantation (for a total of three rounds).

> *Turn the Wheel*
> *Break the cask*
> *Wash away*
> *The thing I ask*
> *[state intent]*

Once the incantations have been completed, hold the mortar in one hand and the pestle in the other. Shake them off at each cardinal point (east, south, west, north) and you say:

> *Carry my desire off to the four winds and return no*
> *more.*

Another use for the mortar and pestle involves the art of counter-magic. The simplest application is known as Quelling. This is designed to put a stop to anything that is set against you. The philosophy of counter-magic is that no one has a right to force you to expend energy defending yourself from an attack (psychic or magical). It is unacceptable to have to feed energy into protective wards because someone is continuing an attack. Therefore, the goal of counter-magic is to cut the attack off at its source—the person or people sending ill intent.

One form of Quelling is to "un-vex" the situation. This not only can stop the negative magical energy from flowing to you, but it also provides for consequences if the person continues. In this way, his or her ill-intended behavior attaches the magic to himself or herself. If the person decides to continue the harmful behavior, then it turns back on him or her, and you no longer have to expend your own energy defending yourself.

The following Quell is designed to stop a person from harming you through deliberate lies, misinformation, and misrepresentation. It can be modified to use for any situation simply by changing the wording. Do not, however, omit the "tapping" of the pestle as the metered sound is important to raising the magic.

Mortar and pestle—Spell of the Quell (the act of un-vexing)

Tapping the pestle back and forth inside the mortar performs this spell. The movement is like a bell clapper swinging inside a bell to make it toll. Use the pestle to keep a slow and deliberate meter as you give the incantation:

> Mark the spirit
> Set the time
> [man/woman] named _____ I here now bind.
> No wagging tongue
> No rolling eyes
> No harmful acts
> No more your lies.
> Wag your tongue—your throat grows sore.
> Roll your eyes—a headache roars.

Harm someone—you grow forlorn.
Spread your lies—you fall on thorns.

Since ancient times, witches have been sought out for casting spells to attract such things as love and prosperity. Witches have also supplied spells to heal, and spells to remove enchantments. The following are some examples of spell casting using the mortar and pestle.

Spell of the Petals (Attracting Love)

On a piece of parchment paper write a description of the ideal mate you desire. It is best not to name an actual person but instead to attract whoever is best suited for a relationship with you. Therefore, write down the character traits, personal nature, and general look you desire. Think in terms of things you desire such as humor, intelligence, personality, compassion, caring, personal grooming, and so forth. If you cannot resist attracting someone you already know of, put his or her photo (or a personal item they have touched) into the mortar along with the parchment paper you wrote on. Include the person's name. After the writing is completed, anoint the paper with your favorite perfume or cologne. You will put it on each day for seven days to empower the spell.

When the description is ready, fold the paper in half and set it down inside the mortar. Drop seven red rose petals into the folded area of the paper. Next, place the end of the pestle over the mortar and rotate it clockwise while saying:

Gather the forces below and above,
bring to me my one true love.
[repeat three times]

Next, gently push the pestle down into the mortar, pressing the paper and rose petals together. Gently grind the paper and petals with the pestle moving clockwise, while saying:

> *Draw together, join together, be together.*
> [Repeat three times]

End the spell by placing the contents of the mortar into moving water such as a stream, river, or ocean. Water is the element of emotion and love. By using this element, your spell is carried into that greater force.

Spell of the Thorns (Severing Love)

On a piece of parchment paper write the name of the person you want to sever your relationship with through this spell. Circle the name and then write yours in another circle next to it (but not touching). Under the other person's name write your intent (think in terms of going away or moving away). Fold the paper and then put it into the mortar. Then drop five rose thorns into the folded area.

Next, place the end of the pestle over the mortar and rotate it counterclockwise while saying:

> *Disperse the forces below and above,*
> *undo the binds that once were love.*
> [repeat three times]

Next, firmly push the pestle down into the mortar, pressing the paper and rose thorns together. Then, tear your name off the paper and remove it (leaving the other person's name behind). Now begin to grind the paper and petals with the pestle, moving counterclockwise, while saying:

> *Repel each other, unlink each other, no longer be the other's.*
> *[Repeat three times]*

End the spell by placing the contents of the mortar into fire. Fire is the element of transformation, and whatever fire touches, it changes into something else. By using this element, your spell is carried into that greater force.

Spell for Prosperity

This spell uses the magical principle of "like attracts like" and the idea of magnetic draw. You will need seven coins that are given to you by someone else. The easiest way to do this is to change a dollar bill into dimes[72] at a store or bank so that you are literally handed the coins. When you return to your work area, select seven of the coins and place them in your mortar. Next, place a loadstone in the mortar. Surround the mortar with rue. Light some incense of a plant or tree nature. Behind the mortar, place three green candles, and light them left to right.

This spell requires circling with the pestle as well as tapping. Begin by running the end of the pestle along the lip of the mortar, clockwise, saying these words:

> *All that I think, do, and say,*
> *increases my finances in every way.*
> *[repeat three this times]*

Next, lift the pestle upward away from the mortar, expanding the clockwise motion out into the area. Say these words:

I raise and expand what here I sow
sevenfold my riches grow.

Now shake the tip of the pestle at each of the cardinal directions and continue the incantation:

I call to the four winds to make it so.

End by circling the pestle down until it touches the mortar again. Then lower it into the mortar and press on the coins three times, saying:

Be the seeds of my financial gain.

Complete the spell by dispersing the coins in an area where people gather (such as a shopping center). Randomly leave a coin here and there. Each time you place one, say:

Return to me a thousandfold.

Walk away and do not look back. The coins will circulate in the flow of exchange through many hands, and this energy will return to you, bringing financial gain.

Spell for Healing
The purpose of this spell is to vitalize and amplify the body's healing abilities. Draw the symbol of the caduceus (the classic symbol

of the medical profession) on a piece of parchment and place it inside the mortar. Surround the mortar with mint leaves (you can tear open some mint tea bags if you don't have access to mint leaves). Place a red candle between two green candles, all set behind the mortar.

Begin the spell by writing the name of the afflicted person on the parchment that is inside the mortar. The name goes just above the top of the caduceus. Below the caduceus (an inch or two) draw a circle and shade it in completely. This represents the illness.

Take the pestle and begin to move it clockwise against the rim of the mortar, and say these words:

> I stir and rally the healing force aglow,
> vitalize the body from head to toe.
> [repeat three times]

Now pick up the parchment paper and fold the area where the shaded circle is drawn (making sure to fold it down and under so that it does not touch the caduceus). Then begin to move the pestle counterclockwise over the rim of the mortar, saying:

> I banish the cause of illness, and all malaise
> weakens and withers with each passing day.
> [repeat three times]

Pick up the parchment paper and carefully cut or tear off the piece with the drawn shaded circle. Set it aside away from your work area. Next, fold the parchment with the caduceus and your name on it, and sprinkle some mint leaves into the fold. Then fold or roll the parchment to encase the mint. Keep this in a red pouch, which needs to be carried by the afflicted person for three days. It can be placed in a pocket or some other area as long as it stays in physical connection.

End the spell by taking the piece of parchment with the circle on it, and piercing this area with a needle seven times. Afterwards, burn the paper with the needle inserted. Take the ashes and blow them into the west, declaring that the illness is banished and cannot return. Clean the needle by boiling it in salted water.

Using the Platter

The platter is a plain light-colored plate about the size of a standard dinner plate. When used, it is covered with sacred ash, and symbols are drawn in the ashes. The platter is, in effect, a ritual book of magical symbols and sigils used for evocation and invocation. Traditionally, whenever an entity or spirit is to be called or worked with, its symbol or sigil is first drawn in the ash that covers the platter. This holds the spirit in place during the rites, which allows it to remain connected with the material realm.

The platter also serves as a banishing or releasing tool. If you rub out the symbol marked in the ash, or blow across it, the symbol disappears. This breaks the link with the spirit or entity. Take this into account if working outside when the wind is blowing.

At the close of any magical or ritual work, return the ash to the pot and wipe the platter clean. Do not retrieve any ash that touches the ground. This is because it loses its force when it touches the earth because its shadow seeps back into the soil.

Concerning Plants and their Spirits

The use of a mortar and pestle naturally indicates the witch's connection to the Plant Realm. As noted earlier, witches can commune with indwelling spirits that are attached to various plants. The magic behind this works through the network of roots that touch the shadow within the earth.

Symbols of the Art

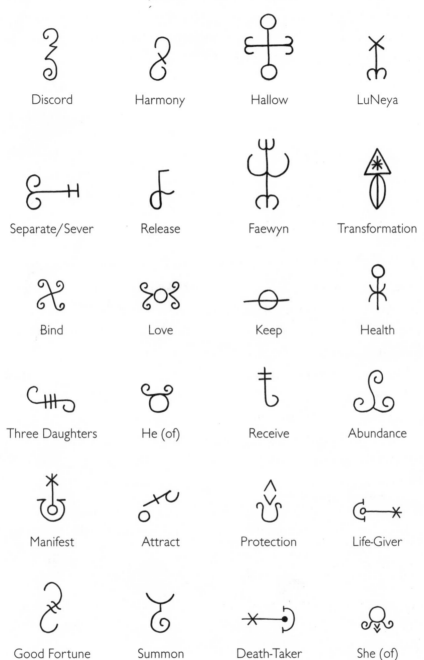

Discord

Harmony

Hallow

LuNeya

Separate/Sever

Release

Faewyn

Transformation

Bind

Love

Keep

Health

Three Daughters

He (of)

Receive

Abundance

Manifest

Attract

Protection

Life-Giver

Good Fortune

Summon

Death-Taker

She (of)

In this section of the Grimoire, we will be working with the spirits of traditional witchcraft plants through the use of magical seals. It is important to understand that working with the actual plants is very dangerous and the odds are high that in doing so you will face dire consequences. Therefore, I have devised a magical system that will make it possible to work with plants and their spirits without having the actual plants they are associated with. To be clear, I am instructing you not to touch, ingest, or inhale any part of the plants included in this book. Use only the plant seals. If you believe anything I say about the magic of plants, then also believe in my warning and comply in accord.

Spell of Personification (The Plant Spirit Seals)

This spell serves to transform a magical seal into the thing it represents. In this way the spirits of the poisonous plants can be called without risking harm from handling the plants. To cast this spell, you need four small bowls and a small cup. One bowl is filled with good soil, one contains smoking incense[73], another contains a lighted candle, and the last bowl is filled with fresh clean water.

Place the bowls in a circular arrangement around the cup with all of them touching it. Etch a triangle around them large enough to enclose all four bowls. The tip of the triangle is arranged to point toward you. Place a lighted candle at each tip of the triangle. These represent the principle of manifestation, which is comprised of three aspects: time, space, and energy. All three must be in force in order for anything to manifest on the material plane.

Draw the desired plant seal on a piece of paper and set it outside the triangle in front of you. Next, hold the seal up and look at the three candle flames, and then say:

Behold the Triangle of Manifestation.

Now, take the paper, with the seal showing, and pass it over each candle flame. Begin with the tip facing you, and then move clockwise. As you pass the seal around the flames, speak these words:

I draw time, space, and energy, joining them as one.

Now you are ready to charge the seal with elemental natures that will create the personification link. You will need to work now with the four bowls. If needed for fire safety reasons, you can spread the triangle candle arrangement out farther. After each incantation, you will sound the tonal associated with the elemental force. These are the vowel sounds: E – I – O – A (stretched out as you sound them).

Beginning with the bowl containing incense, hold the seal over it and say:

I pass to you from the Asthesia the power to call the spirit of this seal of (name plant).
[tonal: Eeeeee]

Next, hold the seal over the bowl containing the lighted candle, and say:

I pass from the Asthesia the power to transform this paper into the active link to the spirit of this seal of (name plant).
[tonal : Iiiiii]

Move the seal over the bowl containing water, and say:

I pass from the Asthesia the power to create movement from
shadow for the spirit of this seal of (name plant).
[tonal: Oooooo]

Hold the seal over the bowl containing soil, and say:

I pass from the Asthesia the power to provide form for the
spirit of this seal of (name plant).
[Tonal: Aaaaaa]

Conclude the spell by holding the seal up as you face the triangle candles, and while looking the seal, say:

By the powers of forces of the Triangle of Manifestation,
I hold the plant in spirit form, and link the entity to this seal.
Spirit of [name plant] you are called by this seal.

Spend a few minutes studying the seal and its symbolism so that the imagery is fully "wired" in the memory center of your brain.

Ritual and Magical Correspondences

1. The Plant Seals

   The designs that comprise the assortment of seals are
   rooted in ancient magical thought. They represent a connection between the image and the associated concept.
   This connection is a means of making contact and drawing
   the awareness of what the symbol is linked to in the greater
   sense. In effect, a seal is a bridge that the consciousness
   uses to close the gap between imagination and realization.

The seals have been designed to depict the blossom of each plant along with a connective symbol associated with its spirit nature. The circle of thorns represents the concept of the "Gate of Thorns" and the "Gathered Thorns" (see Appendix B). The thorn also represents the overseeing plant spirit–She of the Thorn-blooded Rose. Together they link the mystical natures to the material images, which serves to vitalize the seals.

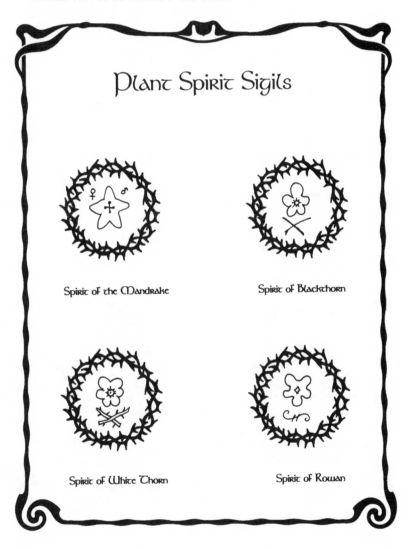

Plant Spirit Sigils

Spirit of the Mandrake

Spirit of Blackthorn

Spirit of White Thorn

Spirit of Rowan

Plant Spirit Sigils

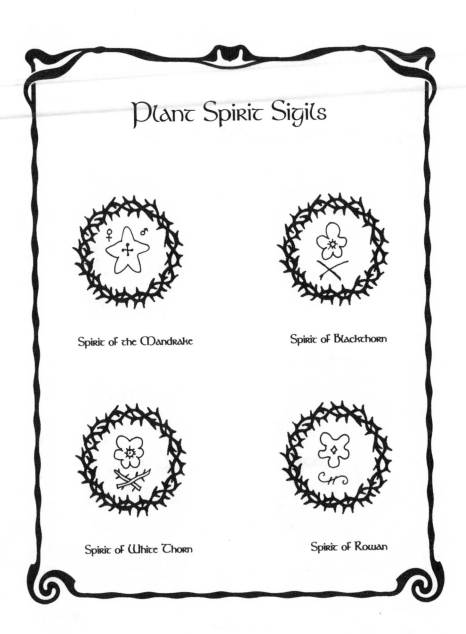

Spirit of the Mandrake

Spirit of Blackthorn

Spirit of White Thorn

Spirit of Rowan

Plant Spirit Sigils

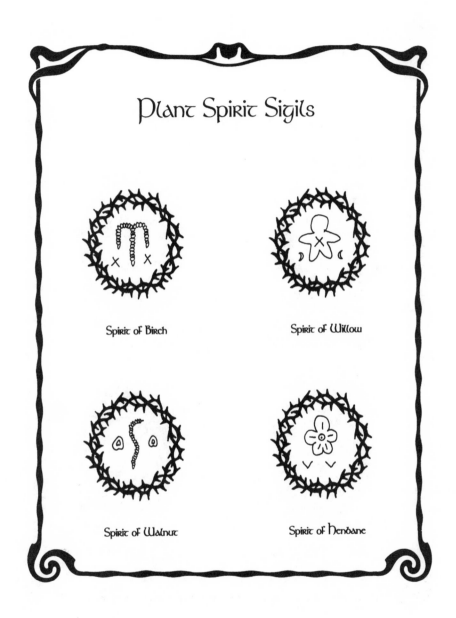

Spirit of Birch

Spirit of Willow

Spirit of Walnut

Spirit of Hendane

Plant Spirit Sigils

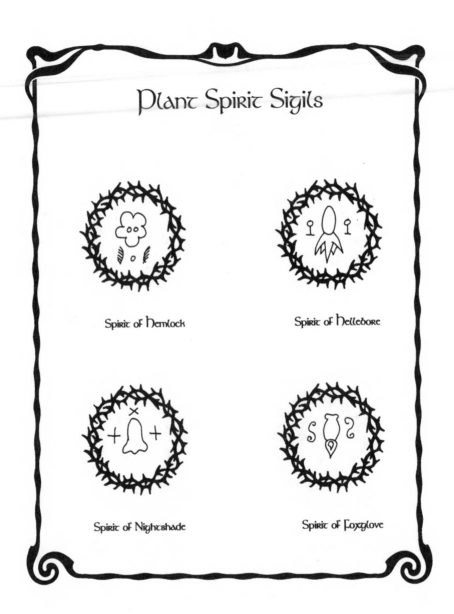

Spirit of hemlock

Spirit of hellebore

Spirit of Nightshade

Spirit of foxglove

2. Parts of the Plant

Root—Command, control, and bind

Crown—Transition and connecting opposites

Stem/Trunk—Changing perspectives, new insights

Leaves—Empowering and energizing

Bud—Opportunities, potential

Flower—Spiritual connections

Fruit—Completion and reflection

Seed—Continuation and preservation

3. Magical Plants

Aconite: works involving Shadow contact

Birch: directing spirits of the dead

Blackthorn: raw power without regulations

Foxglove: summoning Otherworld beings and spirits

Hawthorn: opener of magical doorways and portals

Hellebore: stabilizing and calming situations and spirit activity

Hemlock: reparation and ancestral spirit redemption

Henbane: to block or barrier

Mandrake: mastery

Nightshade: hiding and revealing secrets

Rowan: protection against enchantments

Walnut: achieving goals, fulfilling needs

Willow: binding and oaths

Wolfsbane: banishment

4. Plant Spirits

Atonen: hemlock

Atropa: nightshade

Brydethe: birch

Ellebrina: hellebore

Gebanshen: wolfsbane

Kwethanna: hawthorn

Maestra: aconite

Mandragora: mandrake

Necterra: henbane

Reudwyn: rowan

Sheadwa: blackthorn

Tylanna: foxglove

Wealhenin: walnut

Weligwyn: willow

5. Elemental Correspondences

Earth: associated with the north and with the nature of cohesion. Earth solidifies. Its tonal vibration is the letter A. Its color is yellow for it is influenced by the light and heat of the sun.

Air: associated with the east and with the nature of transmission. Air carries or sends. Its tonal vibration is the letter E. Its color is blue because its agent, the wind, moves through the day sky.

Fire: associated with the south and with the nature of transformation. Fire changes the form of whatever it touches. Its tonal vibration is the letter I. Its color is red.

Water: associated with the west and with the nature of motion. Water takes on the shape of whatever contains it, and it has motion in streams, rivers, waterfalls, and oceans. Its color is green (like a stormy sea).

6. Colors

Black: for works involving potential and multiple possibilities

White: for works of remembrance and preservation

Red: for works of vitality and passion

Blue: for works related to spiritual matters

Green: for works of a fertile or gainful nature

Yellow: for mental stimulation

Brown: for works of neutralizing

Purple: for lunar magic

Gray: for creating a calm balance

Silver: for dream work or envisioning (astral levels)

Gold: for success (material plane)

Working with the Plant Seals

The plant seals can be used to call forth the plant spirits when the plants are not available. This is also a safe way of avoiding contact with the poisonous and toxic properties of traditional witchcraft plants. However, the seals can also be used with the actual plant. This is accomplished by exposing a bit of the plant's root, and then setting the seal so that it makes contact with the root.

The first step in working with the seals is to use the spell of personification. This will create the needed link between you and the spirit. Following this, the seal is placed in front of you on the ground, and an offering is made to the spirit. I suggest using an ounce of liquid chlorophyll mixed with three drops of red wine. After the offering has been made, you can summon the spirit:

> I call to you [name spirit],
> spirit of the [name plant],
> you who aids the witches' craft,
> be favorable to me through this offering,
> and grant my request.
> [state your request]

All that remains now is to design the method of delivering the magical intent to the target. The best method is to pass the magical intent into an object that will come into contact with the target. To do this, temporarily attach the spirit seal to the object for a short period of time or until you are ready to send or place the object.

If the magical intent involves a situation as opposed to a person, place, or thing, then call upon the Asthesia to carry the spell into the astral fabric where it will then manifest in the material dimension. Use the summoning in the Book of Calls, and place the plant seal before you when you call the Asthesia. After they are evoked, you can instruct them regarding what you desire and that you want the intent manifested through their forces.

Apples have long been associated with the Faery Realm and can be used in a variety of ways. One the simplest and most effective methods is to prepare the apple talisman. Take a large apple and slice it horizontally about one third down from the stem area. Then slice a disk from the upper piece, also cutting horizontally. Set this aside for now.

Next, take the apple and core out its center. The idea is to make a bowl out of the apple. This will be used to make offerings to the Faeries. The classic offering consists of equal parts of red wine, honey, and milk. This is called nectar. Some practitioners prefer to offer mead.

The next step is to dry the apple disk. It is best to dry it pressed between two screens (weighted down). This allows the apple to dry evenly and prevents it from curling up into a bow shape. Alternatively, you can wrap it tightly in a paper towel and place over the opening of a cup (not allowing it to fall into the cup).

Once the apple disk is dried, you can write on it with a pen. Write your request around the inside of the outer edge, and add symbols of your intent in the area closer to the core area. Place the apple talisman out with the apple bowl filled with an offering. Do this at night; the night of the full moon is best.

Ghost Stone

To make a Ghost Stone, find a natural stone in or near a grave-yard. You will need to take two small containers of some kind with you. The stone you seek should be no larger than your fist and no smaller than the width of a quarter (coin).[74] In the graveyard locate the oldest tree. Place a coin offering at the base, and then take a piece of its bark from one of the branches. Place the bark in one of the containers and do not let it touch the ground. Next, go to five different areas of the graveyard and scoop some soil near a grave into the other container. Then, leave the graveyard with all the items. Return home to your work area.

If the bark is dry and thick, use a file to grind it into powder. If it is moist and damp, peel it into shreds and leave it to dry for several days. When you have dry bark to work with, place it in the mortar and work the material down by grinding the pestle. The resulting substance is known as graveyard dust.

The soil you have collected is known as graveyard dirt, which is different from dust. The dirt will give you power to temporarily evoke the aid of graveyard spirits. The magical act of using graveyard dirt is known as "calling the five." When working with wayward ghosts you may need assistance.

When you need to charge the stone for magical activation, powder it with a pinch of graveyard dust, and say the following words:

> I call upon She of the Crossroads,
> gatherer and guide of souls,
> you who aids all witchery,
> that through this magical dust
> any spirit must pay heed to the stone
> and comply to my will.

Carry the stone with you when you work with spirits of the dead. Depending on what you encounter, you will use the stone to calm the spirit or relocate the spirit to another place. The proper approach has much to do with understanding why a spirit is haunting an area, what it wants to accomplish, and whether or not it wants resolution. Some spirits simply want to rage or to avenge.

To calm a spirit that wishes release, perform a "funeral rite" and make a mark upon the stone to serve as a headstone. If you do not know the previous religious affiliation of the departed, then draw a skull on the rock. If you have this knowledge, then mark the religious symbol of the faith. Take the stone to the nearest area of soil. Dig a small hole and place the stone at the edge.

Begin the burial with these words:

Peace and release are wished for you,
it is time to pass from this mortal world.
You are free to go, nothing is owed from you.
You will be remembered,
But you must go on now
And begin the spiritual walk ahead.
[pause]
I call for the gateway of light to open
So this spirit may pass through.
[raise arms outward and motion as though parting a curtain]
Pass now in the cares of your guide and guardian.
[spend a few moments envisioning this]

End by filling the hole with the loose soil and place the Ghost Stone as a marker. Place both hands over the "grave" and say: "Go now in peace." Leave the stone in place (you can create another for later use).

You will eventually (if not often) find a spirit that does not want release. It may be a very troublesome spirit that fully intends to continue haunting. If so, you must consider if you really want to be involved in dealing with such a spirit. If you decide to pro-ceed, you will need to direct the spirit into the stone. For this you will need to tie the stone securely to a cord, or place it in a pouch that is secured in this way.

Carry the prepared stone with you as you enter the area of the haunting. There are risks involved in confronting a negative spirit, and you need to be firm and show no fear. When you sense the presence of the spirit, hold the cord with the stone hanging from its end, and address the spirit:

You must leave this place now,
your time in the mortal world has passed.
You disturb the peace of this place and those who live here.
It is not your right to do this. It is their right to live here in
  peace.
It is their time in this world, and this place is their place now.
[Pause and sense the reaction. If the spirit does not leave, then proceed.]
I call upon She of the Crossroads
to take control of this spirit,
and to bring it under my will.

With your dominant hand, start swinging the cord counterclockwise above your head and walk counterclockwise around the room. Speak again:

By the timeless power of the witches' craft,
Spirit, I draw you into the stone.
You have no power to resist.
You are pulled into the stone.

Repeat these words and swing the stone faster. You must stay in a mental frame of power and not waiver. At a point that only you can sense, start to slow down. Eventually bring the stone to a rest. When you do, cup it firmly between your hands and take it outside. Wrap it in a silk scarf to keep any energy from escaping.

In the event that the spirit attacks you when the stone is produced (or at any point), be prepared to defend with the graveyard dirt. To do this, sprinkle five pinches of the dirt on the ground, and say the following lines (one for each pinch):

I call upon five spirits who died unjustly,
I call upon five spirits who died forlorn,

I call upon five spirits who died too soon,
I call upon five spirits who were killed,
I call upon five spirits who died by suicide.
Come now to my aid
And subdue this spirit
And put it in the stone.

Once the spirit is captured in the stone, take it to an uninhabited wooded area far from the place it haunted. Leave it there among the trees and do not return. The stone will keep the spirit bound to this area until it accepts release from the mortal world. This will happen at some point, and out of compassion you should work magic on the spirit's behalf from time to time to aid its release. Work with He of the Deep Wooded Places and She of the White Round to encourage liberation. Eventually the spirit will "climb the branches" to the Otherworld.

Old legends exist about haunted woods, and are often rooted in the binding of wayward spirits to forest places. One superstition included planting a tree on a grave with the intention of keeping the spirit from harassing the living. Townspeople sometimes did this to the graves of people they believed were witches. But as Old Ways witches, we honor the dead and aid them to find release. A permanent binding to the material plane is never acceptable in Old World witchcraft.

Appendix A

THE INVISIBLE GOD
OF WITCHCRAFT

Several years ago I set out to try and discover pre-Christian references to a god of witchcraft. References to various goddesses were plentiful enough, but I found nothing directly revealing a god. Among the earliest goddesses mentioned, the most frequent and prominent are Hecate, Diana, and Proserpina. None of these were connected to any consort in literary sources, and therefore, no trail presented itself that I could follow in search of a god of witchcraft linked to any of these goddesses. It was as though he were invisible.

Hecate is the oldest goddess name associated with witches and witchcraft in Western literature. This fact seemed like a logical place to start the hunt. One of the things that stand out in archaic elements of her veneration is the crossroads. In ancient times a tree trunk called a *hekataion*, which stood in the center of three crossing paths, denoted her presence at the crossroads. In time, the tradition of setting a trunk turned to that of erecting a stone pillar.

Stone pillars set at crossroads became attached to a term known as a *herms*. In its earliest form, it was just a crudely carved column with a square base. Later on, the herms was carved to include a humanoid bust atop the column. The early tradition called for travelers on the roads to leave some collected rocks near the herms. These were in turn used by the road builders to repair and extend the roads. Merchants and suppliers used these roads for commerce.

Surviving images carved on the herms reveal to us that the busts are the gods known as Priapus and Hermes. Of the two, Hermes is connected to Hecate. Both deities are associated with the crossroads, souls of the dead, and passage between the world of the living and the dead. Scholar Karl Kerenyi describes Hecate and Hermes as "secret lovers,"[75] and they share an intimate connection to Otherworld themes. The idea of Hermes in such a close relationship with the classic goddess of witchcraft is very noteworthy.

In his earliest form, Hermes is a god of cattle. These were important animals used in commerce, and so Hermes became connected to commercial ventures. By extension, he was also associated with the roads used for commerce. As a god of cattle, is it possible that the winged helmet we often see him wearing is an image evolved from an earlier crown with two horns? In the earliest depictions of Greek art, it is not clear what the protrusions are on his headwear. However, in later periods they are certainly wings.

In the myths and legends associated with Hermes, we find a magical helmet that makes him invisible. I was intrigued by the idea of an invisible god in light of the fact I could not "see" a god of witchcraft in pre-Christian literature. This motivated me to look further into the nature and character of Hermes.

As I continued my investigation, Hermes began to emerge as an incredibly archaic deity. He is associated with time and with

hermes

the stars. In the book *Hermes, Guide of Souls* by Karl Kerenyi,[76] we find an ancient depiction of Hermes wearing a black cloak covered with stars. He sports a beard and carries a short crook. This is in sharp contrast to the later images in which we find him youthful and clean-shaven.

In the Christian era, Hermes became identified with Satan, perhaps due to his nature as a trickster in ancient myth. Some scholars suggest that the winged devil image of the Middle Ages was inspired by the wings borne by Hermes in Greek art. The Devil's pitchfork may also be derived from the caduceus held by Hermes, which resembles a trident. Hermes is associated with escorting souls of the dead to the Underworld, and the Devil is depicting as ensnaring them and holding them in hell.

Among the interesting connections to Hermes is the advent of musical instruments. In one tale he invents the lyre for Apollo and the flute for Pan. This is noteworthy in light of a continuing superstition among musicians. An old custom is to go to the crossroads and make a deal with the Devil in exchange for increased musical talent. As noted earlier, Hermes is intimately connected to the crossroads. Is this a coincidence?

Near the end of my search for pre-Christian references to a god of witchcraft, I remembered a curious image. It is not from this early period, but it bears a symbol that cannot be ignored. The image is that of the Sabbatic Goat, also known as Baphomet. Upon examining the figure, a phallus is clearly present and is in the form of the caduceus of Hermes. Could the Sabbatic Goat be a form of Hermes associated with witchcraft? When we factor in that one of Hermes's cult animals is a goat, the question becomes more intriguing.

In previous chapters we noted that witches reportedly gathered to commune with spirits of the dead at the crossroads. Hermes is also a god of communication and messages. In ancient times Hecate and Hermes were the primary deities connected to the setting of the crossroads and the theme of spirit contact. Hecate is the Gatekeeper to the Underworld, and Hermes is the escort of the dead. What better deity to call upon when working with invisible spirits of the dead than an invisible god?

Appendix B

THE FIVE-THORNED PATH

The Five-Thorned Path

The rose flower has long been one of the symbols of inner groups and secret societies. In fact, the Latin term *sub rosa* (meaning under the rose) is used to denote secret teachings or communication. This is one of the reasons the rose appears in the initiation rites of Old World witchcraft.

The thorns of the rose symbolize several things including perseverance through challenges. They are also associated with blood lineage, the ancestral connection of the witch. Witches are keepers of the blood mysteries, and the thorn draws forth blood, which is symbolic for all keepers of the "river of blood" that flows from our ancestors and pulsates in our bodies.

The "mystery training" system within Old World witchcraft is known as the Five-Thorned Path. It encompasses five components of magical training and five elements of spiritual connection, and the tips of a five-pointed star represent each one. However, the symbol is not intended to represent a star per se. It is instead a configuration of five red thorns around a black center in the shape of a pentagon.

The thorns represent the "blood passion," and each one symbolizes one component of training in the mystical system. The black center represents the magical concept of *Shadow*. The latter is a force beneath the earth that retains the *memory* of all living things that have existed on the earth. This memory passed into the soil as each living thing was absorbed. We can liken this concept to the Eastern Mysticism concept of the Akashic Records, which are said to be astral memories on a higher plane. As above, so below.

The positioning of the thorn pentagram differs according to two different aspects. One position represents the spiritual path of training, and the other represents the mastery of the arts of witchcraft as a magical system. The thorn pentagrams are not elemental pentagrams with element nature assignments to each area. Even though the orientation of the tips does change, the symbol is not thought of as upright or inverted.

In formal design, the base of each thorn touches the center figure of the pentagon they surround. This connects them to Shadow. The starlike symbol featuring one thorn on top represents the journey of the soul in each incarnation as a witch. It is called the *Gate of Thorns*. The circle enclosing the group of thorns symbolizes the wheel of birth, life, death, and rebirth.

In operation, the top thorn represents the realm of the stars, our cosmic origin. We follow this down to the bottom right thorn. This symbolizes the solar imprint, which is known as the birth chart in astrology. The upper left thorn represents the lunar or astral realm in which the soul is prepared and passed into a mortal vessel. The upper right thorn is the material world but, more precisely, the land on which we are born. This ties us to the *spirit of the land*, which stays with us in each lifetime. The lower left thorn symbolizes our attachment to the spirit of *shadow*, which teaches us the ways of the witch and the ways of our ancestors. The black pentagon in the center represents our flow downward into Shadow, the joining to the group mind of all who came before us.

When we view the starlike thorn pattern with two thorns on top, it represents the development of the witches' power within the mortal realm. The symbol is called the *Gathered Thorns*. Each thorn represents one of the five powers of the witch. The circle enclosing the thorns symbolizes the full moon as well as the wheel of the moon through each monthly journey.

Beginning with the lower left thorn, we note the connection to the plant kingdom. This marks the witch as the magical herbalist, the knower and tender of plants. The upper right thorn symbolizes oracle ability (a seer in possession of divination skills). The bottom thorn is the connection to the Underworld and spirits of the dead. This is the ability of the witch to speak with the dead.

The thorn on the upper left symbolizes the witch as a mystic, one who can traverse into other realms of existence. The lower right thorn represents the forces of magic, the witch as the sorceress or sorcerer.

The black pentagon in the middle of the thorns symbolizes the upward flow of the Shadow force, its extension to the witch. Shadow can pass its hidden knowledge to the witch. This is not only through the sharing of memory, but also in conjunction with plant spirits. The teaching is that each type of plant possesses a spirit. The roots of the plant literally tap into Shadow and draw upon the imbedded memory. This memory is, in part, contained within the decomposed elements within the soil.

Notes

Preface

1   One example is the execution of a woman condemned by the Inquisition in Milan (1390) for "attending an assembly" led by Diana (Kieckhefer, *European Witch Trials*, 117).

Chapter One

2   Gordon, Richard. "Imagining Greek and Roman Magic," in Ankarloo, Bengt and Stuart Clark, eds., *Witchcraft and Magic in Europe, Vol. 2: Ancient Greece and Rome* (University of Pennsylvania Press, 1999), 251.

3   Circe first appears in writings attributed to Homer, which date around 800–700 BCE. By some accounts, she appears to be a goddess and in others a witch. However, she is always depicted as mortal and capable of being slain by a physical weapon. This portrayal undermines support for her goddess nature, but does lend support to her depiction as a witch.

4   Gordon, Richard. "Imagining Greek and Roman Magic," in Ankerloo and Clark, eds., *Witchcraft and Magic in Europe, Vol. 2: Ancient Greece and Rome* (University of Pennsylvania Press, 1999), 50.

5   Duni, Matteo. *Under the Devil's Spell: Witches, Sorcerers and the Inquisition in Renaissance Italy* (Syracuse University, 2007), 53.

6   Simpson, Michael. *The Metamorphoses of Ovid* (University of Massachusetts Press, 2001), 113.

7   Witch Hunter Francesco Guazzo, in his seventeenth-century work titled *Compendium Maleficarum*, writes that "witches observe various silences, measurings, vigils, mutterings, figures and fires, as if they were some expiatory religious rite." (Chapter 11, page 123).

8   In the story, the writer tells us that Circe used a spell to force him into an intimate relationship. However, Ulysses spent the previous ten years in a foreign land involved in the Trojan war. Having not been with a woman for ten years, it is unlikely that a spell was necessary to evoke his passion. But, in the story it does conveniently serve to justify his adulterous behavior and vilify the witch.

9 Ankarloo and Clark. *Witchcraft and Magic in Europe, Vol. 2: Ancient Greece and Rome*, 184, 204.

10 Duni. *Under the Devil's Spell*, 28.

11 Russell, Jeffrey. *The Devil: Perceptions of Evil from Antiquity to Primitive Christianity* (Cornell University Press, 1977), 170.

12 Filotas, Bernadette. *Pagan Survivals, Superstitions and Popular Cultures* (Pontifical Institute of Mediaeval Studies, 2005), 19.

13 Birnbaum, Lucia Chiavola. *Black Madonnas: Feminism, Religion & Politics in Italy* (iUniverse, 2000), 17.

14 Ibid.

15 Martin, Ruth. *Witchcraft and the Inquisition in Venice 1550–1650*. (New York: Basil Blackwell Inc., 1989).

16 *The Catholic Encyclopedia*, volume 2 (The Encyclopedia Press, Inc., 1913), 478.

Chapter Two

17 Kieckhefer, Richard. *European Witch Trials: Their Foundation in Popular and Learned Culture, 1300–1500*. (University of California Press, 1976), 2.

18 Cohn, Norman. *Europe's Inner Demons: The Demonization of Christians in Medieval Christendom* (University of Chicago Press, 1993), 163.

19 Ibid.

20 Gordon. "Imagining Greek and Roman Magic," 96.

21 Ravenwolf, Silver. *Solitary Witchcraft* (Llewellyn Publications, 2003), 29.

22 Cohn. *Europe's Inner Demons*, 164.

23 Ibid., 167.

24 Ginzburg, Carlo. *Ecstasies: Deciphering the Witches' Sabbath* (Random House, 1991), 90.

25 Peters, Edward. *The Magician, the Witch, and the Law* (University of Pennsylvania Press, 1978), 92.

26 Kors, Alan C., and Peters, Edward. *Witchcraft in Europe 1100–1700* (University of Pennsylvania Press, 2001), 149.

27 *www.beyond-the-pale.org.uk/zxMassa.htm* (accessed for research 8/11/10).

28 Mormando, Franco. *The Preacher's Demons* (University of Chicago Press, 1999), 66.

29   Stephens, Walter. *Demon Lovers: Witchcraft, Sex, and the Crisis of Belief* (University of Chicago, 2002), 132. Passavanti mentions the Devil deceiving non-witches but does not directly connect witches and the Devil together.

30   MacFarlane, Alan. *Witchcraft in Tudor and Stuart England* (Waveland Press, 1970), 6.

31   Hole, Christina. *Witchcraft in England* (B.T. Batsford, Ltd., 1947), 130.

32   In chapter one we noted this same tactic used against the witches Medea and Circe.

33   The most common translation of this title is *The Night Meetings of Witches*. However, the word *lammie* actually refers to an evil night spirit that became associated with the witch figure. Tartarotti may have used it in the title because of its colloquial relevance in his time period.

34   Tartarotti, Giralomo. *Del Congresso Notturno delle Lammie* (Gia M. Batista Pasqua, Libraro e Stampatore, 1749).

35   Burne, Charlotte. *Shropshire Folklore* (Trubner and Co., 1883), 143.

36   Michelet, Jules. *La Sorciere: The Witch of the Middle Ages* (Simpkin, Marshall and Co., 1863), 1.

37   Carpenter, Edward. *Intermediate Types among Primitive Folk: A Study in Social Evolution* (Mitchell Kennerley, 1914), 51–52.

38   It is interesting to note an entry in *The Oratorical Dictionary*, by John Newland Maffitt (W. Cameron Printer, 1835). The word Pythoness is defined as: A witch; the priestess of Delphi in Greece (page 246).

39   Gage, Matilda Joslyn. *Woman, Church and State: A Historical Account of the Status of Woman through the Christian Ages.* (The Truth Seeker Company, 1893), 134.

40   Hueffer, Oliver Madox. *The Book of Witches* (1908), 53–54.

Chapter Three

41   Several nineteenth-century folklorists performed independent field studies on witchcraft in different regions of Italy. The most noted were J.B. Andrews, Roma Lister, Lady De Vere, and Charles Godfrey Leland. They interviewed people who self-identified as witches (*streghe*) and collected data that were almost identical. All the studies pointed to family traditions in which witchcraft was passed through the female members.

42   The Italian Inquisitor Arnaldus Albertinus, in his work titled *Tractatus de agnoscendis assertionibus catholcis, et hereticis* (circa 1540), claimed that witches are called *strigae* because they communicate at night by screaming like screech owls.

43   Doniger, Wendy, and Yves Bonnefoy. *Roman and European Mythologies*. (University of Chicago Press, 1992), 46.

44   Ankarloo and Clark. *Witchcraft and Magic in Europe, Vol. 2: Ancient Greece and Rome*, 184.

45   Pócs, Éva. *Between the Living and the Dead* (Ceu Press, 1999), 50.

46   One example is an accused witch names Antonio Corregi circa 1595. He reportedly healed people by passing them three times through a freshly split nut tree.

47   Davies, Owen. *Witchcraft, Magic, and Culture 1736–1951* (Manchester University Press, 1999), 175.

48   Ibid., 168.

49   Ibid., 180.

50   Ryan, Meda. *Biddy Early: The Wise Woman of Clare* (Mercier Press, 1991), 9.

51   Gordon, Lina. *Home Life in Italy: Letters from the Apennines* (The MacMillan Company, 1908), 238–40.

52   Andrews, J. B. "Neopolitan Witchcraft," in Transactions of the Folklore Society, Vol. 3, No. 1 (1897).

53   A funerary tradition involves birch dolls of this fashion being suspended from tree branches or placed in tree hollows in an old belief that this aids rebirth of the departed soul.

54   On a side note ancient philosophers such as Plutarch and Plato mention the shadows on the moon and refer to them as the caverns of Hecate or Proserpina. In period tales the dead dwell in these caverns.

55   Gimbutas, Marija. *The Language of the Goddess* (Harper San Francisco, 1991), 251.

56   Hesiod's writings are the earliest mention of Hecate, and he is the first to put oral tradition into print in southern Europe.

57   Heaton, Eliza Putnam. *By-Paths in Sicily* (E.P. Dutton & Company, 1920), 28.

58   In the book *Witchcraft: A Tradition Renewed,* by Doreen Valiente and Evan Jones, there is a passage on page 54 addressing the relationship between the Horned God, the Dying God, the Divine King, and the Devil. The latter is depicted as the living representative of the cult figure. This may be the root of the legend of the Black Man who appears in old witchcraft lore.

59   One legend claims that Cain was the son of Lilith, and Abel the son of Eve. This suggests a possible rift between Cain and Abel that may have

caused ill feelings between the two brothers. In the biblical tale God favors Abel but is displeased with Cain. Here we have a thread suggesting that Lilith's son is not equal to Eve's son in the eyes of God.

60   Leland, Charles Godfrey. *Aradia or The Gospel of the Witches* (1899), 1.

61   In the 1960s the words *witch* and *Wiccan* were interchangeable. Over time, along with different generational views, the notion of Wicca as the religion of witches came into being. At this phase, witchcraft became the practice of the magical arts. In turn, with all the changes, witches and Wiccans were seen as not necessarily being the same people.

62   This is the "outer court" name for what is known only to initiates. *Outer court* is a term used to denote what can be revealed in a public manner.

63   Messina, Christine. *Cinderella and Other Classic Italian Fairy Tales* (Children's Classics, 1993), xii.

Chapter Four

64   Jones, Roger Miller. *The Platonism of Plutarch* (George Banta Publishing Company, 1916), 48–53.

65   Philpot, J. H. *The Sacred Tree in Religion and Myth* (MacMillan and Co., Ltd., 1897), 82, 133.

66   The witch stands between the forces of day and night, and thereby becomes the third element in this magic. From here she or he directs the flow, in essence taking on the classic form of the Magician in the Tarot.

67   In a way, divination is like forecasting the weather. Patterns and currents are examined in order to forecast the probable outcome, but forces may intervene that change direction and formation. This applies equally to foreseeing the future. It is the gift of divination that we can be made aware of what is forming in the future. From this knowledge we can then make choices and direct our lives as need be.

Chapter Five

68   Davies, Owen. *Grimoires: A History of Magic Books* (Oxford University Press, 2009), 41.

69   Summers, Montague. *History of Witchcraft and Demonology.* (Citadel Press, 1993), 86–87.

70   From the book *The Italian Novelists* (The Facetious Nights of Straparola), by W. G. Waters. Privately published for members of the society of bibliophiles, London, 1901, page 12.

71   Bosca, Donato. *Masca ghigna fàussa. Il mistero delle streghe piemontesi dalla veglia contadina all'analisi sociologica* (Priuli & Verlucca 2005).

72   Many years ago dimes were imprinted with the image of Mercury as the god of commerce, and were therefore known as Mercury dimes. They have been used in spell casting ever since. For a special and potent connection, you can purchase Mercury dimes in a coin shop. They are a treasure.

73   Put some sand in the bowl to burn charcoal on or to stand an incense stick in.

74   You may want to take more than one stone as in the workings the stone is left behind. If you have only one stone, then you will have to return to the graveyard to resupply.

Appendix A

75   Kerenyi, Karl. Hermes, *Guide of Souls* (Spring Publications, 2008), 84–85.

76   Ibid., frontispiece.

Bibliography

Ankarloo, Bengt, and Stuart Clark, eds. *Witchcraft and Magic in Europe, Vol. 2: Ancient Greece and Rome*. Philadelphia: University of Pennsylvania Press, 1999.

Ankarloo, Bengt, and Gustav Henningsen, eds. *Early Modern European Witchcraft: Centres and Peripheries*. Oxford: Clarendon Press, 1993.

Benko, Stephen. *The Virgin Goddess: Studies in the Pagan and Christian Roots of Mariology*. Leiden: Brill Academic Publishers, 2003.

Beyerl, Paul. *A Compendium of Herbal Magick*. Custer: Phoenix Publishing, Inc., 1998.

Birnbaum, Lucia Chiavola. *Black Madonnas: Feminism, Religion, & Politics in Italy*. New York: iUniverse, 2000.

Bosca, Donato. *Masca ghigna fàussa. Il mistero delle streghe piemontesi dalla veglia contadina all'analisi sociologica*. Sarmagno: Priuli & Verlucca 2005.

Breslaw, Elaine, ed. *Witches of the Atlantic World: An Historical Reader and Primary Sourcebook*. New York: New York University Press, 2000.

Burne, Charlotte. *Shropshire Folklore*. London: Trubner and Co., 1883.

Carpenter, Edward. *Intermediate Types among Primitive Folk: A Study in Social Evolution*. New York: Mitchell Kennerley, 1914. Reprint, General Books, LLC, 2009.

The Catholic Encyclopedia, volume 2. New York: The Encyclopedia Press, Inc., 1913.

Cohn, Norman. *Europe's Inner Demons: The Demonization of Christians in Medieval Christendom*. Chicago: The University of Chicago Press, 1993. Revised edition.

D'Alton, John Francis. *Horace and His Age: A Study in Historical Background*. London: Longmans, Green and Co., 1917.

Davies, Owen. *Grimoires: A History of Magic Books*. New York: Oxford University Press, 2009.

————. *Witchcraft, Magic and Culture 1736–1951*. Manchester: Manchester University Press, 1999.

Doniger, Wendy, trans., and Yves Bonnefoy, comp. *Roman and European Mythologies*. Chicago: The University of Chicago Press, 1992.

Duni, Matteo. *Under the Devil's Spell: Witches, Sorcerers and the Inquisition in Renaissance Italy*. Florence: Syracuse University, 2007.

Eliade, Mircea. *Occultism, Witchcraft, and Cultural Fashions*. Chicago: The University of Chicago Press, 1976.

Filotas, Bernadette. *Pagan Survivals, Superstitions and Popular Cultures*. Toronto: Pontifical Institute of Mediaeval Studies, 2005.

Folkard, Richard. *Plant Lore, Legends, and Lyrics: Embracing the Myths, Traditions, Superstitions, and Folk-Lore of the Plant Kingdom*. London: Sampson, Low, Marston & Company, 1892. Reprinted by General Books, LLC. 2010.

Friend, Hilderic. *Flower Lore*. Rockport: Para Research, Inc., 1981.

Gage, Matilda Joslyn. *Woman, Church and State: A Historical Account of the Status of Woman through the Christian Ages*. New York: The Truth Seeker Company, 1893. Reprinted by Persephone Press in 1980.

Gardner, Gerald. *The Meaning of Witchcraft*. New York: Samuel Weiser, 1976.

————. *Witchcraft Today*. New York: Citadel Press. 1970.

Gibson, Marion. *Reading Witchcraft: Stories of Early English Witches*. London: Routledge, 1999.

Gimbutas, Marija. *The Language of the Goddess*. New York: HarperCollins, 1991.

Ginzburg, Carlo. *Ecstasies: Deciphering the Witches' Sabbath*. New York: Random House, 1991.

Gordon, Lina. *Home Life in Italy: Letters from the Apennines*. London: The MacMillan Company, 1908.

Harrison, Michael. *The Roots of Witchcraft*. London: Tandem Books, 1973.

Heaton, Eliza Putnam. *By-Paths in Sicily*. New York: E.P. Dutton & Company, 1920.

Hole, Christina. *Witchcraft in England*. London: B. T. Batsford, Ltd., 1947.

Jones, Roger Miller. *The Platonism of Plutarch*. Menasha, WI: George Banta Publishing Company, 1916.

Kerenyi, Karl. *Hermes, Guide of Souls*. Woodstock: Spring Publications, 2008.

Kieckhefer, Richard. *European Witch Trials: Their Foundations in Popular and Learned Culture, 1300–1500*. Berkeley: University of California Press, 1976.

Kittredge, George Lyman. *Witchcraft in Old and New England*. New York: Atheneum, 1972.

Klaniczay, Gábor, and Éva Pócs, eds. *Witchcraft Mythologies and Persecutions (Demons, Spirits, Witches; vol. 3)*. New York: Central European University Press, 2008.

Kors, Alan C., and Peters, Edward. *Witchcraft in Europe 1100–1700*. Philadelphia: University of Pennsylvania Press, 2001.

Larner, Christina. *Witchcraft and Religion: The Politics of Popular Belief*. Oxford: Basil Blackwell, 1984.

Lavender, Susan, and Anna Franklin. *Herb Craft: A Guide to the Shamanic and Ritual Use of Herbs*. Freshfields: Capall Bann Publishing, 1996.

Lindsell, Harold, ed. *Harper Study Bible*. Grand Rapids: Zondervan Bible Producer, 1962.

MacFarlane, Alan. *Witchcraft in Tudor and Stuart England*. Prospect Heights: Waveland Press, 1991.

Martin, Ruth. *Witchcraft and the Inquisition in Venice 1550–1650*. New York: Basil Blackwell Ltd.,1989.

Messina, Christine. *Cinderella and Other Classic Italian Fairy Tales*. New York: Children's Classics, 1993.

Michelet, Jules. *La Sorciere: The Witch of the Middle Ages*. London: Simpkin, Marshall and Co., 1863.

Monther, E. William. *European Witchcraft*. New York: John Wiley & Sons, Inc., 1969.

Mormando, Franco. *The Preacher's Demons*. Chicago: University of Chicago Press, 1999.

Murray, Margaret A. *The Witch Cult in Western Europe*. New York: Barnes & Noble, Inc., 1996.

Newall, Venetia. *The Witch in History*. New York: Barnes & Noble Books, 1996.

Notestein, Wallace. *A History of Witchcraft in England from 1558 to 1718*. New York: Thomas Y. Crowell Company, 1968.

Ogden, Daniel. *Night's Black Agents*. New York: Continuum US, 2008.

Peters, Edward. *The Magician, the Witch, and the Law*. Philadelphia: University of Pennsylvania Press, 1978.

Philpot, J. H. *The Sacred Tree in Religion and Myth*. London: MacMillan and Co., Ltd., 1897.

Pócs, Éva. *Between the Living and the Dead*. Budapest: Ceu Press, 1999.

Porteous, Alexander. *The Forest in Folklore and Mythology*. New York: Dover Publications, Inc., 2002.

Purkiss, Diane. *The Witch in History: Early Modern and Twentieth-Century Representations*. London: Routledge, 1996.

Ravenwolf, Silver. *Solitary Witchcraft*. Woodbury: Llewellyn Publications, 2003.

Russell, Jeffrey. *The Devil: Perceptions of Evil from Antiquity to Primitive Christianity*. Ithaca: Cornell University Press, 1977.

Ryan, Meda. *Biddy Early: The Wise Woman of Clare*. Blackrock: Mercier Press, 1991.

Schulke, Daniel A. *Viridarium Umbris: The Pleasure Garden of Shadow*. Worchestershire: Xoanon Publishing, 2005.

Simoons, Frederick J. *Plants of Life, Plants of Death*. Madison: University of Wisconsin Press, 1998.

Simpson, Michael. *The Metamorphoses of Ovid*. Amherst: University of Massachusetts Press, 2003.

Stein, Rebecca L. and Philip L. *The Anthropology of Religion, Magic, and Witchcraft*. Boston: Pearson Educational, Inc., 2005.

Stephens, Walter. *Demon Lovers: Witchcraft, Sex, and the Crisis of Belief*. Chicago: University of Chicago, 2002.

Summers, Montague. *History of Witchcraft and Demonology*. New York: Citadel Press, 1993.

Tartarotti, Giralomo. *Del Congresso Notturno delle Lammie*. Venice: Gia M. Batista Pasqua, Libraro e Stampatore, 1749.

Valiente, Doreen, and Jones, Evan. *Witchcraft: A Tradition Renewed*. Custer: Phoenix Publishing Inc., 1990.

About the Author

 Raven Grimassi is a Neo-Pagan scholar and award-winning author of more than fourteen books on witchcraft, Wicca, and Neo-Paganism. He has been devoted to the study and practice of witchcraft for over forty years. Raven is co-founder and co-director of the Fellowship of the Pentacle, a modern Mystery School tradition of pre-Christian European beliefs and practices.

Grimassi's background includes training in old forms of witchcraft as well as Brittic Wicca, the Pictish-Gaelic tradition, and Celtic Traditionalist Witchcraft. Raven has also been a member of the Rosicrucian Order and studied the Kabbalah through the First Temple of Tifareth under Lady Sara Cunningham. His early magical career began in the late 1960s and involved the study of works by Julius Evola, Franz Bardon, Gareth Knight, Kenneth Grant, Dion Fortune, William Gray, Austin Osman Spare, William Butler, Israel Regardie, Eliphas Levi, and William Barrett.

Grimassi currently lives in New England with his beautiful wife and co-author Stephanie Taylor-Grimassi. He enjoys such things as collecting Silver Age comics featuring Dr. Strange, working in the herbal garden, and occasionally relaxing on the porch with a nice cigar on a warm summer night.

Visit him online at: *www.ravengrimassi.net*

To Our Readers

Weiser Books, an imprint of Red Wheel/Weiser, publishes books across the entire spectrum of occult, esoteric, speculative, and New Age subjects. Our mission is to publish quality books that will make a difference in people's lives without advocating any one particular path or field of study. We value the integrity, originality, and depth of knowledge of our authors.

Our readers are our most important resource, and we appreciate your input, suggestions, and ideas about what you would like to see published.

Visit our website *www.redwheelweiser.com* where you can subscribe to our newsletters and learn about our upcoming books, exclusive offers, and free downloads.

You can also contact us at *info@redwheelweiser.com* or at

Red Wheel/Weiser, LLC
665 Third Street, Suite 400
San Francisco, CA 94107

299.94 G861   HJUNW

Grimassi, Raven,

Old world witchcraft :ancient ways

for modern days /
JUNGMAN

04/12

DISCARD